The Illustrated Bede

John Marsden is the author of a number of books on the early history of Scotland and Northumbria and now makes his home in the Western Isles. His *Illustrated Life of Columba* and *Sea-Road of the Saints* are also published by Floris Books.

John Gregory is the author of *The Neoplatonists* (1991) and has recently completed a new translation of Josephus' *Life of Herod*. His translation of Adamnan's *Vita Columbae* is published in *The Illustrated Life of Columba* and extracts from his translation of Bede have been broadcast on BBC Schools Radio. He holds degrees from the universities of Cambridge, London and Durham, and now lives in North Yorkshire.

Geoff Green lives in York. His photography has also been published in *The Illustrated Life of Columba* and elsewhere, notably in the new guidebook to St Paul's Church at Jarrow.

The Venerable Bede

This modern sculpture of Bede, carved from elm wood
by Fenwick Lawson and based on a medieval portrait
from the Engelberg Codex, stands under the tower arch
in St Paul's Church, Jarrow.

The Illustrated Bede

John Marsden

Translation by John Gregory
Photography by Geoff Green

Floris Books

First published in 1989 by Macmillan, London.
This revised edition first published in 1996 by Floris Books.

British Library CIP Data available

ISBN 0-86315-226-0

Printed in Great Britain
by The Bath Press, Bath

Contents

ORKNEY

DALRIADA

IONA

Antonine Wall

STRATHCLYDE

LINDISFARNE

BERNICIA   Bebbanburg
            BAMBURGH

            In Gyruum
            JARROW

Hadrian's Wall   Wiuraemuda
                  MONKWEARMOUTH

NORTHUMBRIA

MAYO

White House
(Candida Casa)
WHITHORN

DEIRA

Eboracum
YORK

Inisboufind
INISHBOFFIN

Dearmach
DURROW

LINDSEY

GWYNEDD

Beardaneu   Peartaneu
BARDNEY   PARTNEY

Maserfelth
OSWESTRY

In Undalum   EAST
OUNDLE

MERCIA   Elge
              ELY

Grantacaestir   ANGLIA
CAMBRIDGE

Dorciccaestra   Verulamium
DORCHESTER   ST ALBANS

Hrofaescaestir
ROCHESTER

WESSEX   KENT   Rutubi
        SUSSEX   Portus
                             RICHBOROUGH

Acknowledgements

The author and photographer are grateful to the following for their
generosity and cooperation in allowing photography for this book:

Bede's World (formerly The Bede Monastery Museum), Jarrow
Beverley Minster
The Dean and Chapter of Durham Cathedral
St John's Church, Escomb
The Dean and Chapter of Ely Cathedral
The Rector, Hexham Abbey
English Heritage
The Iona Cathedral Trust
St Paul's Church, Jarrow
St Peter's Church, Monkwearmouth
The National Trust
The Dean, Cathedral and Abbey Church of St Alban

The author would also like to add a personal note of
thanks to Miss Susan Mills of Bede's World, Mr Billy Shiel of Seahouses,
and Miss Marjorie Tomlinson of St Albans for their special assistance
along the way to *The Illustrated Bede*.

Dedicated to the memory
of Edward Peel Hutton

Preface to this Edition

It is said of the scribes of Bede's time that they would always leave some detail of their manuscript books less than perfectly finished in recognition of their belief that only God was able to produce the perfect completed work. As far as I can recall some seven years after the event, there was no such intention on the part of the author, translator and photographer of the original edition of *The Illustrated Bede*, but some errors did, nonetheless, find their way into the finished book. If for that reason alone, I was determined to do all I was able to arrange for the publication of a new and corrected edition of the book and I am especially grateful to Christian Maclean and Christopher Moore at Floris Books for their having made it possible.

It is tempting for an author contemplating a new edition of an earlier book to want to revise, rewrite, and even reconstruct the whole thing, but *The Illustrated Bede* was so generously received by so many readers on its first appearance that I thought it best to resist any such temptation. The text and translation, then, remain substantially unchanged, with only a few points of detail amended. The design of the book and its illustrations, however, did need revision to accommodate its new softback format and, in so doing, it has been possible — largely through the cooperation of Miss Susan Mills of Bede's World — to include colour illustrations of folios from the famous 'Leningrad' manuscript of Bede's *Historia* which were not available for use in the first edition.

Having stood beside the marble tomb in the Galilee Chapel at Durham more than once in recent years and promised to put matters right one day, I can only hope now that this reappearance of *The Illustrated Bede* might, at least in some small measure, further encourage the ever wider appreciation of this most remarkable man of Northumbria's Golden Age.

JM, 1996

INTRODUCTION

Bede in his time

To look back at the time of Bede is to peer through the misted prism of almost thirteen centuries at the Northumbria of the late seventh and early eighth centuries AD.

Bede lived at the mid-point of the epoch so long referred to as the 'Dark Ages,' traditionally the centuries of savagery and the sword between the leaving of the legions and the arrival of the Norman conqueror on the Sussex coast in 1066.

The surviving legacy of those distant centuries includes the riches of the Sutton Hoo ship-burial and the splendour of the Lindisfarne Gospels, reflecting the polarity of the times in the symbolic figures of royal warlord and monastic scribe.

Yet nothing of that legacy can match the enduring importance of a book written by a monk of Jarrow in the third decade of the eighth century. Bede's *Historia Ecclesiastica Gentis Anglorum* — his *Ecclesiastical History of the English People* — was the first recognizable attempt at a written history of England. Its pages offer a unique chronicle of these islands from the Roman conquest to the decades that preceded the first onslaught of the Vikings.

This great history was the work of one remarkable man, a scholar monk of the north country who is revered still as the father of English history. Yet Bede was also a poet and musician, a scientist and theologian. He was very probably the most learned man in the Europe of his time and he remains today one of Northumbria's greatest sons.

Northumbria in Bede's time far outreached the county boundaries of modern Northumberland. Its name — deriving from the Anglo-Saxon 'be northan Hymbre' — means 'the land north of the Humber.' It was the vast landmass that stretched from the marshlands of Humberside across fen, forest and fell to its northern frontier on the banks of the Forth. Across this wild, bleak countryside — a landscape well fitted to the 'wyrd' of Saxon legendry — the principal thoroughfares were still the roads built for the soldiery who garrisoned the Roman Wall. Barely three hundred years after the last legions had abandoned that northern frontier, the settlements that had grown up in the shadow of the *Pax Romana* remained.

The enduring evidence of Roman building in stone — lighthouses on the coast and signal stations inland, forts and mile-castles along the serpentine length of the Wall — would have provided prominent land-marks. The great Cheviot dominated the landscape then as it does today, and the ancient igneous rock of the Great Whin Sill formed the natural fortress outcrop at Bamburgh — from where two kings of Northumbria laid claim to rule the whole of Britain — and the Farne Islands a few miles out to sea from that splendid coastline that Sir Walter Scott de-scribed as 'Northumbria's lordly strand.'

The people of this land of Northumbria, Bede tells us, were predomi-nantly the English. These 'English' were Germanic tribes of Angle — rather than Jute or Saxon — stock who had arrived on these shores during the course of the previous two centuries, some as mercenaries recruited to fight in the Romano-British wars and others who came to raid, invade and conquer the land abandoned by Rome.

Bede writes of four peoples in these islands, of which the indigenous Britons and the newly settled English were two. To the north were the Picts, like the Britons native to their land. To the west the Irish had expanded from Ireland to settle the western seaboard of Scotland and establish their kingdom of Dalriada. By Bede's time, the Picts, the Irish and the British dwelt on the western and northern fringes of a land dominated by the Anglo-Saxon English.

Thus the seven kingdoms of the Anglo-Saxon heptarchy — Kent, Sussex, Wessex, Essex, East Anglia, Mercia and Northumbria — vied for dominance of all Britain. On various momentous occasions there emerged a warrior king from one or another of these seven kingdoms whose power was such as to justify the stature of *Bretwalda*, the 'ruler of Britain.' Bede's history lists seven kings mighty enough to hold the standing of *Bretwalda*. Aelle of the South Saxons was the first, followed by Caelin of Wessex and Aethelbert of Kent; the fourth was Raedwald of the East Angles and the last three were all kings of Northumbria, Edwin of Deira and Oswald and Oswy, brothers of the royal house of Bernicia.

The kingdom of Northumbria spanned and on occasions united the territory of two sub-kingdoms. The kingdom of Deira was the elder of the two, emerging from its obscure origins on the northern bank of the Humber estuary. The royal house of Bernicia dominated the northern reaches from the fortress at Bamburgh, where Ida the warlord had landed in 547. Ida's dynasty was to dominate Northumbria's history for more than two hundred years. It was Ida's son, Aethelric, who first united the kingdom of Northumbria, and Aethelric's son, Aethelfrith, who turned his sword-point north towards the ancient domain of the Britons and the Picts.

The resurgence of Deira came when Edwin — in alliance with Raedwald — overwhelmed Aethelfrith in battle on the river Idle and brought Northumbria under Deiran rule. In his turn, Edwin — the first Northumbrian *Bretwalda* — was brought down by the onslaught of Penda of Mercia and Cadwalla of Gwynedd. With the defeat of Edwin the royal house of Deira lost its dominance and the Northumbrian power centre was to shift henceforth to the royal fortress at Bamburgh.

Northumbria disintegrated into a divided kingdom, governed by two sub-kings far too weak to resist the ravages inflicted by the conquering Penda and Cadwalla. Northumbria was only to rise again when Oswald, the son of Aethelfrith, returned to crush Cadwalla's Welshmen at Heavenfield. Oswald was succeeded as *Bretwalda* by his brother Oswy, who finally brought down Penda in battle on the river Winwaed. Bede will provide us with his own chronicle of the triumphant reign of Oswald and the turbulent years of Oswy.

Christian kings had ruled in Northumbria since the baptism of Edwin into the faith on Easter Day in the year 627. By the time of Bede's birth almost fifty years later, Christianity was firmly established in the north country.

The first Christians to reach Northumbria were Romans who brought the new faith from the heart of the Empire to the Wall on its northern frontier; but to seek out the more immediate origins of the northern church in Bede's time we must look to the seaboard of Dalriada, where

BRITANIA

Oceani insula cui quondam albion
nomen fuit inter septentrionem
et occidentem locata est germaniae
galliae hyspaniae maximis euro
pae partibus multo interuallo ad
uersa. quae per milia passuum
dccc in boream longa latitudinis
habet milia cc exceptis dum taxat
prolixioribus diuersorum promon
toriorum tractibus quibus efficitur
ut circuitus eius quadragies octies
lxxv milia conpleat. habet a meri
die galliam belgicam cuius proximi
litus transmeantibus aperit ciuitas
quae dicitur rutubi portus, a
te anglorum nunc corrupte repta
caestir uocata, inter quem ponto mari
adhriomald morinorum gentis
litore primo. traiectu milium l
siue ut quidam scripsere stadiorum
ccccl. a tergo autem unde oceano
infinito patet orcadas insulas ha
bet

Opima frugibus atque arboribus insula.
et alendis apta pecoribus ac iumentis
uineas etiam quibusdam in locis ger
minans. sed et auium ferax terra
marique generis diuersi fluuiis quoque
multum piscosis ac fontibus praeclara
copiosis. et quidem praecipue issicio
abundat et anguilla. capiuntur
autem saepissime et uituli marini.
et delfines nec non et ballenae. exceptis
uariorum generibus conchyliorum.
in quibus sunt et musculae quibus inclusam
saepe margaritam omnis quidem
coloris optimam inueniunt. id est et
rubicundi et purpurei et hyacinthini
et prasini sed maxime candidi.
et cocleae satis superque habundan
tes quibus tinctura coccinei coloris
conficitur. cuius rubor pulcherrimus
nullo umquam solis ardore nulla
ualet pluuiarum iniuria pallescere
sed quo uetustior eo solet esse uenustior.
Habet fontes salinarum. habet et
fontes calidos et ex eis fluuios bal
nearum calidarum. omni aetati
et sexui in per distincta loca iuxta
suum cuique modum accommodos.
aqua enim ut sanctus basilius dicit
feruidam qualitatem recipit. cum per
certa quaedam metalla transit
currit. et fit non solum calida sed
et ardens quae etiam uenis metal
lorum aeris ferri plumbi

the Irish holy man Columcille beached his coracle on the sands of Iona in 565.

Columcille — or St Columba as he is remembered — was a proud and awesome figure, a prince who might have become a high king of Ireland had he not chosen to follow the priesthood. He established a Celtic church on Iona that exerted a dominant influence far beyond the islands and highlands of Dalriada, even as far as that other holy island of Lindisfarne.

If we disregard the legends of Joseph of Arimathea at Glastonbury, it was only in 597 — the year of Columba's death — when Pope Gregory's emissary, Augustine, came to Kent that Christianity reached the southern kingdoms of Anglo-Saxon England. His Kentish church flourished in the south and only ventured north when Edwin's Kentish queen brought the priest Paulinus to Northumbria. In his church raised on the Roman foundations of Eboracum at York, Paulinus baptized Edwin and his royal household. The ferocious onslaught of Penda and Cadwalla that brought Edwin's reign to its bloody end forced Paulinus to flee back to Kent with the widowed queen, and pagan gods ruled briefly again in the north country until the coming of Oswald in 634.

Oswald, who had found sanctuary on Iona as a boy after the defeat of Aethelfrith, had been educated in the Christian faith on Columba's island. Consequently, his allegiance was to the Irish tradition of Iona rather than to the Roman orthodoxy of Kent, and it was to Iona he turned for the man to restore the faith to his kingdom.

Thus came the Irish bishop Aidan to Lindisfarne. The forty years between Aidan and Bede saw the foundation of the great sequence of Northumbrian monasteries from Coldingham down to Whitby. But the Church history of those decades was dominated as much by bitter controversy as by the founding of monasteries. We shall hear much from Bede of the great divide between the Celtic and Roman orthodoxies and its resolution in council at Whitby. Whatever cultural strains of the ancient Irish tradition endured, even reflected in Bede's own history, the Celtic Church had retreated from Northumbria almost a decade before Bede, and the Roman orthodoxy was — formally at least — in the ascendant.

Such were the land and the people, the church and the state, in the Northumbria of Bede's time. Let us turn now to the great scholar monk himself.

The slender core of what we know of Bede is to be found in the last pages of his *Historia Ecclesiastica Gentis Anglorum*. There he provides a brief note of autobiography in which he tells us that he 'was born on the lands of this monastery' of Wearmouth/Jarrow and 'at the age of seven was entrusted ... to the reverend Abbot Benedict, and then to Ceolfrith to be educated.' Since that time he had lived his whole life in that monastery 'devoting myself entirely to the study of the scriptures.'

'Britannia Oceani insula cui quondam Albion nomen fuit'

Decorated initial page at the beginning of Book I of Bede's *Historia Ecclesiastica* from the manuscript now known as the 'Leningrad Bede,' which was written at Wearmouth/ Jarrow and very possibly during Bede's lifetime.

M. E. Saltykov-Schedrin Public Library, St Petersburg: MS lat Q.v.I.18, f.3v

Some attempt to read between Bede's lines may tell us a little more of his beginnings. At the time of his birth, most probably the year 673, Benedict Biscop established his monastery of St Peter on land at the mouth of the river Wear granted to him by King Egfrith, who had succeeded his father Oswy in 671. Some years later — after Bede had been taken into the community at Wearmouth — Egfrith granted further land to Abbot Benedict at Jarrow for a second monastic house dedicated to St Paul. Bede himself recognized both monasteries as houses of one monastic foundation, but at the time of his birth the 'lands of this monastery' were at Wearmouth and not yet at Jarrow. This must cast some doubt on the tradition that his birthplace was Monkton, a village some two miles from Jarrow where a wishing-well has long been known as 'Bede's Well.' If Bede was born on the lands of Biscop's monastery then his birthplace must have been close by Wearmouth.

We can be more precise when we look at Bede's words translated into the English of Alfred the Great's time. Bede's Latin *natus in territorio eiusdem monasterii* is rendered into Anglo-Saxon as *accenned on sundurlonde pas ylcan mynstres.* The Anglo-Saxon word *sundurlond* or *sundorland* means 'land set apart,' effectively estates granted for the support of a monastery. Bede's Wearmouth — known today as Monkwearmouth — has long been swallowed up by the modern town of Sunderland, and it is surely not stretching the Anglo-Saxon translation too far to suggest that the name Sunderland must derive from that 'land set apart' for Biscop's first monastery.

Some distance up the north-east coast from the mouth of the Wear, the village of North Sunderland lies just inland from the harbour at Seahouses. The few miles of coast between Seahouses — originally quite literally the 'sea houses' of North Sunderland — and Bamburgh includes a cluster of buildings at the edge of the beach known for centuries as Monks' House. Traditionally this was the site of storage buildings used by the monks of Lindisfarne to supply the island hermitage on Inner Farne.

Inner Farne served as a retreat for Aidan and afterwards as a hermitage for Cuthbert and those later brothers who followed his example. The lands around Monks' House were probably granted to Lindisfarne — possibly as early as the time of Aidan — as 'land set apart' for the monastery. 'Sundurlonde' again ... hence the village of North Sunderland, just south of Monks' House and a few miles down the coast from the royal capital at Bamburgh.

If Bede was born on 'the lands of this monastery' as they stood in the year of his birth, we can reasonably claim Sunderland as his birthplace.

We do not know whether Bede's parents commended their seven-year-old son to the care of the monastery to be trained as a priest, or simply for his general education at a time when a monastery was the only place where a youngster could gain any kind of academic schooling.

We do know that their choice of Bede's place of education was an extremely fortunate one. Benedict Biscop's monastery was well appointed as a place of learning. The library — gathered by its abbot in the course of his extensive continental travels — was unrivalled in seventh-century England. The young Bede already had the Anglo-Saxon equivalent of unlimited access to the Reading Room of the British Library.

Bede spent two years in the monastery at Wearmouth, but he probably saw very little of the much-travelled Abbot Benedict, who was so often away on his journeys gathering books and treasures from the continent. Bede's tutor from his earliest days in the monastic life was certainly Ceolfrith, Biscop's principal assistant at Wearmouth.

When Egfrith made a further grant of land — this time a few miles to the north at Jarrow — to Biscop's foundation, Ceolfrith was appointed the first abbot of the new monastery dedicated to St Paul.

The nine-year-old Bede accompanied Ceolfrith to Jarrow, where the second monastic house of the dual foundation of Peter and Paul rose up beside the river Tyne. Like St Peter's at Wearmouth, St Paul's at Jarrow was built 'in the Roman manner' of mortared stone. Much of that stone would have been found, already dressed for building, in the abandoned Roman fort at nearby South Shields close to the eastern end of the Wall.

By the year 685 the Jarrow monastery was completed and ready for dedication. Bede was almost certainly in attendance on the day the dedication stone was laid, and that same stone — its carved lettering still clearly legible — can be seen in the wall above the entrance to the Saxon chancel of today's church of St Paul at Jarrow.

Barely a year after that service of dedication, disaster fell heavily on both houses of Benedict Biscop's foundation. The founder himself was far away on a journey to Rome. He left Ceolfrith as abbot at Jarrow and raised the monk Eosterwin to become abbot at Wearmouth. From an anonymous *Life of Ceolfrith* — probably the work of one of Bede's pupils — we learn the details of the terrible plague that swept through the monasteries. Eosterwin himself fell victim and died of the pestilence at Wearmouth. The community at Jarrow was decimated and the anonymous chronicler tells how only Abbot Ceolfrith and a solitary young boy survived to sing the services at the appointed hours of the monastic day. There is no certain evidence that that solitary surviving boy was the twelve-year-old Bede, but it does seem very likely and perhaps it was his characteristically self-effacing humility that prevented his describing his undoubtedly courageous role through those dark days of the plague in his *Lives of the Abbots*.

The monastery at *In Gyrwum*

A model of St Paul's monastery at Jarrow in Bede's time from Bede's World, Jarrow. Viewed from the south, the two church buildings stand behind the living quarters and refectory of the monastic community. The gardens lay between the monastic quarters and the river, while the larger building on the river bank was probably a workshop.

OPPOSITE

'At the age of seven I was entrusted by the care of my family to the reverend Abbot Benedict and then to Ceolfrith ...'

The west porch at St Peter's Church, Monkwearmouth. It was through this porch — dating from the foundation of St Peter's monastery in 673 — that the boy Bede would have passed to begin his monastic career.

The unknown chronicler tells how the strain on Ceolfrith and the boy Bede of singing all the offices of the day became so great that Ceolfrith reached a point where he was forced to sing only the psalms and to omit the customary antiphons. But his piety soon compelled him to restore the antiphonal responses and the complete offices were again sung at Jarrow through the remaining days of the pestilence.

We can draw from this account evidence that the young Bede was already a church musician of unusual education and substantial proficiency. The learning of the psalms was considered an important part of the monastic education. St Wilfrid, when a boy at the monastery on Lindisfarne, won great acclaim for the speed with which he learned the entire psalter by the age of fourteen.

Bede's musical interests must have been greatly inspired by the visit to Wearmouth of Bishop John, the celebrated arch-cantor of St Peter's in Rome. It is no small tribute to the importance of Biscop's foundation that so renowned an ecclesiastical musician was prepared to make so long and arduous a journey. John's visit to Wearmouth first introduced the plain-song technique of Gregorian chant to the English church.

The terrors of the plague and the inspiration of so remarkable an introduction to church music aside, there is little reason to imagine that Bede's early years at Wearmouth and Jarrow were greatly different from those of any other boy in a monastic community of the time. The monastic life was dominated by discipline and order. The daily round of communal prayer began with matins — sometimes as early as two in the morning — and ended with compline in the late afternoon or early evening. The remaining hours of the day were passed in study, contemplation and manual labour. There was corn to be threshed and winnowed, livestock to be fed and fish to be caught. The brewing of mead and growing of herbs were activities of especial importance at Jarrow, while the kitchens and bakehouse provided their own round of daily tasks. A contemporary source tells us that simple but wholesome food was served in the monastic refectory. Fish — always a prominent item on the menu at Jarrow — and flesh meats, kitchen herbs and beans, butter and cheese were washed down with ale when it was available and water when it wasn't.

A reference in Bede's own introduction to his metrical *Life of Cuthbert* offers first-hand evidence that he suffered from some form of speech impediment or infirmity of the tongue until it was healed through the miraculous intervention of St Cuthbert. Writing around the year 716, Bede refers to the numerous miracles attributed to Cuthbert and tells us that 'there is one of these ... I experienced myself through the healing of my speech while I was singing of his miracles.' Some modern scholarship has suggested that Bede was writing metaphorically of being inspired to poetic achievement by Cuthbert's miracles, but two medieval chroniclers take Bede's reference quite literally. Symeon of Durham, historian of the Lindisfarne community's journey with Cuthbert's coffin, quotes Bede's remark and the later Reginald of Durham, in his twelfth-century account of beneficiaries of Cuthbert's miracles, records that 'one of their number was the renowned teacher Bede who merited to be freed ... from an impediment of speech.' It does seem likely that Bede did suffer from some such affliction, probably throughout his early years at Wearmouth and Jarrow.

The rapid progress of Bede's monastic career suggests that his outstanding qualities were already clearly in evidence as he reached manhood. His own autobiographical note records that he was ordained deacon at the age of nineteen; and when Abbot Ceolfrith called on Bishop John of Hexham — the future St John of Beverley — to ordain Bede no less than six years before the customary age required by canon law, he offered clear recognition of his pupil's extraordinary learning and dedication.

Bede goes on to record that he was ordained priest at the age of thirty, and once more Bishop John carried out the ceremony. 'Since then,' he writes at the end of the *Historia*, 'I have lived my whole life in this monastery, devoting myself entirely to the study of the scriptures and amid the observance of the Rule and the daily task of singing in the church, it has always been my delight to learn, to teach or to write.'

Between his entering the monastery in 680 and his death in 735, Bede travelled no further than Lindisfarne and York. William of Malmesbury's claim that Bede paid a visit to Rome has not a shred of evidence to support it. Pope Sergius did invite a company of monks from Jarrow to Rome in 701, but there is no indication that Bede — then not yet a priest — was among their number.

It is widely accepted that Bede paid at least one visit to Lindisfarne, probably to offer a first draft of his prose *Life of Cuthbert* for approval by the Lindisfarne community who had commissioned the work and to complete his researches into Cuthbert's life at first hand. If such were the case, his visit would have been made no later than 721, when he was almost fifty.

A letter from Bede, written only two years before his death, is addressed to Egbert, his former pupil who became bishop of York and tutor of Alcuin. Bede refers to his recent visit to York at Egbert's invitation and declines a further invitation on the grounds of his failing health.

If it seems strange that so renowned a scholar and historian should have been so modest a traveller, it is important to remember that Bede's home was the great centre of civilization of his time. The foundation of Wearmouth/Jarrow was splendidly furnished and appointed by the standards of the time. Italian paintings of sacred and scriptural subjects hung on the walls. Windows glowed bright with coloured glass produced by craftsmen brought from Gaul. The buildings were walled 'in the Roman manner' with mortared stone and floored with a concrete of powdered brick and pebble. Vessels and candlesticks of silver would have stood on the altars at both monasteries and a cross of gold was one of the treasures at Wearmouth.

Wearmouth and Jarrow may have fallen short of the grandeur of St Wilfrid's great churches at Hexham and Ripon, but nowhere in England could rival the magnificent library assembled by Benedict Biscop and expanded by Ceolfrith. Here Bede was surrounded by all the great works of classical authors and contemporary scholars. The writings of Pliny and Virgil stood beside the letters of Pope Gregory the Great, the cosmography of Isidore of Seville and St Jerome's translation of the gospels. The flow of distinguished visitors and extensive correspondence with other monastic houses would have brought news from the world outside, but it was Biscop's great library which encompassed the world of Bede the scholar monk.

The scriptorium of Bede's monastery was of equal, indeed complementary, importance to the library. In Bede's time the only technique of book production and text reproduction was the handwriting of the scribe. A book would be acquired — by loan, gift or purchase — for the library of a monastery and then a copy, or copies, would be made by the brothers in the scriptorium. In a dual foundation such as Wearmouth/Jarrow, a book acquired by one house would be copied for use by the other.

The scriptorium of Wearmouth/Jarrow enjoyed great distinction. There is nothing to confirm whether each house had its own scriptorium or where a single scriptorium might have been sited to serve both houses. There is extensive manuscript evidence to show how Wearmouth/Jarrow developed its own distinctive calligraphic style. Its uncial script was derived from continental manuscripts brought back by Benedict Biscop and developed into the elegant hand found in the pages of the great *Codex Amiatinus* in Florence and the leaves of the 'Ceolfrith Bible' in the galleries of the British Library.

This uncial script offers interesting comparison with the insular hand of the Lindisfarne scribes. Uncial did not have the freedom of the insular hand and certainly took longer to execute. In the eighth century, when the Wearmouth/Jarrow scriptorium was under increasing pressure — largely because of demand for the works of Bede — the insular hand came into more regular use by virtue of its greater speed. The two earliest surviving Wearmouth/Jarrow manuscripts of Bede's *Historia* are written in the insular hand, while uncial was apparently reserved for the copying of scriptural texts. The work of the scriptorium must have provided long and painstaking labour for even the most skilled and dedicated monastic craftsman and the production of books in this fashion was also an expensive business.

The quill pens used by the scribes were easily come by in such places as Wearmouth, Jarrow and Lindisfarne where the local bird-life would provide an abundant supply of feathers to be shaped into the scribe's quill. The horns of bulls could be fashioned into sturdy wells for the ink, which was probably made from soot or lampblack. The vellum parchment was prepared from calf, sheep and goat hides, dried, stretched and smoothed in readiness for the scribe's ink-laden quill. A manuscript of some two hundred and forty leaves would have required the skins of between a hundred and a hundred and twenty animals to provide its vellum.

All the surviving examples of Wearmouth/Jarrow manuscripts, apart from scriptural texts, are the works of Bede. His own bibliography, which follows his autobiographical note in the *Historia*, lists some forty works. Many of them were written in more than one volume and together they cover scholarly interests that range from hagiography — the chronicling of saintly lives and works — to natural science.

Bede's first book on chronology, *De Temporibus*, was written at the time of his ordination as a priest and his study of 'the nature of things,' *De Natura Rerum*, was written around the same time. Like the chapter of topography that opens the *Historia*, these books are drawn from Bede's researches into the books of the classical scholars with the illuminating addition of examples from his own observations. A second work on chronology, *De Temporum Ratione*, was written at much the same time as he was working on his great history. Questions of chronology were of great importance and no less controversy in Bede's time. He was writing only a few decades after the Council of Whitby had reached its momentous decision between the Roman and Celtic orthodoxies on the dating of Easter.

Bede's chronological writings were intended to support the dominant Roman orthodoxy, but perhaps an aspect of greater interest today is his use of the 'Anno Domini' system of dating which he derived from the work of Isidore, bishop of Seville. The BC/AD system of chronology was effectively Isidore's invention, but Bede was certainly the first to develop it for use in the writing of history. Bede's scientific writings, like all his works, had an essentially educational purpose and were primarily intended for use as textbooks in the monastery.

All the surviving works of Bede are written in Latin, but he also read Greek and Hebrew and wrote in the Anglo-Saxon vernacular. He translated the *Paternoster* and the *Credo* for use by non-Latinists, and was completing an English translation of St John's Gospel at the time of his death. He wrote poetry in both Latin and Anglo-Saxon, and his Latin poems alone, many of them lyrics intended to be sung in church, fill some hundred octavo pages. Bede's *Martyrology* was compiled in his later years and became the model from which all later western Church calendars have descended. It was written at the instigation of his friend Acca, an enthusiastic collector of tales of martyrdom who succeeded St Wilfrid as bishop of Hexham.

By the standards of modern scholarship, Bede might seem to be largely a transcriber of other scholars' work, but such activity was the nature of the scholarship of his time and Bede is the outstanding exception in that he subjected his primary sources to careful scrutiny and drew extensively on his own observations and first-hand information.

He was always willing to quote directly — and sometimes without identifying his source — from other writers whose work he believed to be reliable and this has been of some value to modern historians. By piecing together a jigsaw of Bede's literal quotations it has been possible to construct a list of the books from which he worked in the library of Wearmouth/Jarrow and the languages of which he had a command.

Bede was first and foremost a priest. All his scholarly work was based on a religious and moral intent. His writings on chronology and natural science sought to reveal the mind of God in the natural world, while his history and hagiography sought to reveal the hand of God in the affairs of men. Even Bede's primers on grammar and spelling drew their examples from scriptural texts.

It is true that without Benedict Biscop's library and scriptorium there could have been no Bede the scholar monk, but it is also true that the relatively peaceful history of his own times made its own contribution to his scholarly achievement. Had he been born half a century earlier Bede would have found himself at the mercy of the warriors of Penda and Cadwalla. If he had been born much more than fifty years later, he would have been working on his *Historia* when the devastating Viking raids fell on the monasteries of Northumbria in the last decade of the eighth century.

The kings who ruled Northumbria through Bede's own lifetime presided over almost a century of relative peace. Egfrith succeeded his father the *Bretwalda* Oswy in 671, just a few years before Bede's birth. Egfrith was much in the mould of the warrior king, yet he was also a substantial benefactor of the Church. Guided no doubt by his saintly queen, Etheldreda of Ely, Egfrith granted the lands for Biscop's foundation first at Wearmouth and later at Jarrow.

Egfrith was succeeded by his half-brother Aldfrith, the illegitimate offspring of a liaison between Oswy and an anonymous princess of an Irish royal house. Educated on Iona as the pupil of its abbot Adamnan, Aldfrith was more monk than king. He eagerly granted more lands to the monastery of Wearmouth/Jarrow in exchange for a copy of a book on cosmography for his own library, and it has been claimed that it was Aldfrith who first wrote down the Anglo-Saxon oral epic of *Beowulf.*

On the death of Aldfrith, his son Osred — a vicious young man remembered as the rapist of nuns — succeeded and ruled until his own death in mysterious circumstances at the age of nineteen. Cenred and Osric — both of them suspected of dark involvement in Osred's death — ruled successively and in equal obscurity at Bamburgh until 729. Osric was succeeded by Ceolwulf, who resembled Aldfrith in his monkish inclinations — so much so that shortly after his accession he was seized by his nobles to be forcibly and scornfully tonsured. Ceolwulf nevertheless ruled until the year 737, when he finally abdicated to spend the remaining twenty-seven years of his life as a monk on Lindisfarne.

It was to Ceolwulf that Bede dedicated his great *Historia Ecclesiastica Gentis Anglorum,* written in the last decade of his life and completed about AD 731. It offers a chronicle in five books of eight hundred years of history, and to find a comparable work before Bede we must look back — as he did — to the historians of classical antiquity. After Bede no comparable historian emerged in this country until William of Malmesbury wrote his *Gesta Regum Anglorum* at the end of the eleventh century.

It is an impressive fact that Bede's great history has been read and revered — first in Latin, then in Anglo-Saxon, and eventually in modern English — for more than twelve hundred years. The earliest surviving manuscripts — written in the scriptorium of Wearmouth/Jarrow, possibly during Bede's own lifetime — have long been the subject of study and speculative discussion by palaeographers and historians. Probably the oldest, certainly one of the two oldest, is the manuscript in Leningrad, taken there by a British diplomat as a gift to Russia in the eighteenth century. The date AD 746 appears in its pages, but scholars have suggested this was a slightly later addition to the original manuscript, much of which has been shown to be the work of at least one scribe who was a contemporary of Bede.

The other early *Historia* manuscript is kept rather nearer home in the Library of Cambridge University. This is the manuscript known as the 'Moore Bede' in recognition of its one-time owner, Bishop John Moore of Ely. To judge by the calligraphic execution and hurried correction of errors, this is the work of a scribe of considerable skill working under some pressure. The demand for copies of Bede's work began towards the end of his life and escalated dramatically thereafter, prompting the use of the more swiftly executed insular hand in the scriptorium. Those factors date the Moore manuscript to shortly after Bede's death, or at the earliest shortly before it.

Copies were transcribed in Bede's Latin for a hundred years. An

especially handsome manuscript — once thought to have been of Lindisfarne but now believed to have been written in southern England, possibly at Canterbury, and only a few decades after Bede's death — is to be seen in the galleries of the British Library. A century after Bede, it was Alfred, the greatest of Anglo-Saxon kings, who directed the translation of the *Historia* into the English of his time, acknowledging it as one of the books 'most necessary for all men to know.' The *Anglo-Saxon Chronicle* draw on Bede's history as does almost every historian of medieval and later centuries.

The first translation into recognizable modern English was that of Thomas Stapleton, who dedicated his work to the reigning Elizabeth I. Stapleton's text was the first edition of Bede's history to benefit from the new technology of printing, on the press of John Laet of Antwerp in 1565.

By that date, the *Historia* was already more than eight and a half centuries old. Since then it has undergone a sequence of translations that have each enjoyed the increasing advantages of ever greater archaeological and historical research. It remains today one of the outstanding documents of the English heritage.

The stature of Bede's history is well established, and his own standing as a historian is no less remarkable. He derived material from the books of other scholars, but always carefully compared and evaluated the texts on which he drew. He extended them with his own contributions and took every opportunity to draw on first-hand sources among his contemporaries. He questioned Bishop Wilfrid on the sensitive question of St Etheldreda's virginal state, because Wilfrid had been her personal counsellor. He drew on Abbot Berthun's personal recollections of his predecessor, St John of Beverley. He consulted the brothers on Lindisfarne to prepare his accounts of St Cuthbert. The many distinguished and informed visitors to Jarrow were surely closely questioned by the resident historian for details to supplement his reading in the library and the correspondence with other monasteries to which he often refers in his text.

Bede's techniques of historical research reflect his place at the meeting point of the intellectual traditions of his time. Learned in Latin and in Greek, he was able to draw on classical and continental authors. Yet Bede was an Anglo-Saxon, a direct heir to the great oral tradition that has passed down to us *The Wanderer*, *The Seafarer* and *Beowulf* from their origins among the bards of the mead-halls of the ancient northern world.

'In an age when little was attempted beyond the registration of fact,' writes the eminent authority on Anglo-Saxon England, Sir Frank Stenton, 'Bede had reached the conception of history.' Bede marks the starting point of a long line of great English historians. Without him we would know only a fraction of the story of the early middle ages, of the golden age of Northumbria, and of the first centuries of the Church in these

'Britain is an island in the Ocean, and was once called Albion'

The Northumberland coast, near Craster.

islands. He stands today as the first English historian, the unrivalled father of English history.

Perhaps the one most disconcerting aspect of Bede's history for the modern reader is the realization that a time-honoured and authoritative work of historical record describes a miracle on virtually every page. Bede tells of scrapings from the leaves of Irish manuscripts offering a cure for snakebites, of saints who regularly heal the lame and restore the sight of the blind, quell storms and quench fires, of divine visions prophesying death and saintly corpses lying for decades incorrupt in their tombs. This is not something which readers of A.J.P. Taylor or Lord Macaulay are accustomed to find in works of history.

The great Bedan scholar Bertram Colgrave suggests that it would have been just as extraordinary for Bede to have omitted the miraculous as it would for similar supernatural phenomena to feature prominently in a modern work of history. Bede was writing nearly a thousand years before the dawn of scientific enlightenment. He was writing for an audience who had moved only within living memory from belief in the rune-working of Woden and the fate-weaving of the Wyrd. Bede was a man of his time and the supernatural was a powerful component in the culture of that time. The miraculous was at least as historically important for Bede as was the rise and fall of any warrior king.

In the same way that Bede's historical scholarship draws inspiration from several cultural traditions, so his theological position is fortunately placed. Even a casual reading of his ecclesiastical history reveals him as a committed advocate of the Roman orthodoxy that had triumphed over the Celtic cause at Whitby. There is no reason to suspect Bede's commitment to the Roman way, and yet his regard for the ancient Celtic tradition that swept so dramatically from Ireland and Iona to Lindisfarne remains every bit as passionate as his somewhat more formal obeisance to the orthodoxy of Rome.

Bishop Hensley Henson of Durham, writing over fifty years ago, describes Bede's relationship to divergent traditions of faith and learning in a paragraph that is in itself an evocative portrait miniature of the scholar monk of Jarrow:

> The more closely Bede's career is studied, the more amazing it appears. He stood at the point of a new departure — a Bened-ictine monk in the yet living tradition of Celtic piety, an English student in the rich treasury of Celtic learning, a disciple of Rome inspired by the intellectual passion of Ireland.

'An Island in the Ocean'

When Bede began his great *Historia Ecclesiastica* with an outline of the physical and human geography of Britain, he was simply following the tradition of those authors of classical antiquity whose works served as the model for his own, and yet in doing so he displayed his own awareness of the importance of the geographer's science for the historian.

Bede's opening chapter on 'the situation of Britain and Ireland and their earliest inhabitants' is a remarkable document. It is the work of a monk of Northumbria who had travelled no further than the Holy Island of Lindisfarne some fifty miles up the coast from his monastery at Jarrow. It was not until AD 733, two years after the completion of the *Historia* and two years before his death, that Bede journeyed as far south as York, known to him as the Eboracum of the Romans.

Map-making was unknown in eighth-century Northumbria, and the great library of Wearmouth and Jarrow is not known to have contained maps, atlases or gazetteers. Bede draws on classical topographers to estimate the coastline of Britain at some 4,875 miles. Modern geographers, making allowance for the movement of tides, suggest a figure of something over 4,900 miles. Bede's margin of error is impressively slim for a monastic historian working from ancient texts almost thirteen centuries ago.

The splendid library assembled by Benedict Biscop and Ceolfrith provided Bede with his primary sources in the works of such as Pliny, Isidore of Seville and the British historian Gildas. Bede drew extensively on such writings, but he added much of his own. He had no need to venture far into the world when so much of the world came to Jarrow.

There are clues in these pages that reveal something of Bede himself and his perspective through the windows of Jarrow. He makes mention of the quality of 'grazing for cattle and draught animals' but goes into much greater detail about the fish, shellfish and other creatures of the sea. Such a zoological imbalance should come as no surprise from a writer who had lived all his years on the North Sea coast in a monastery whose community we know fed principally on the harvest of the sea.

When Bede wrote of Spain, he was writing of the land of the sixth-century Isidore of Seville, whose encyclopedia was certainly in the library of Wearmouth and Jarrow, but when he wrote of Gaul he was writing

of a land well known to his first abbot, Benedict Biscop, who brought masons from that country to build monasteries in the Roman manner.

Adamnan, abbot of Iona and biographer of Columba, made at least two visits to Northumbria, bringing to Bede's monastery first-hand accounts of that island which was for so long the heartland of the Celtic tradition. But when Bede wrote of Ireland, his respect and awe knew no bounds. There is no reference to Irish pagan history and legend in his description of a wholly Christian land 'rich in milk and honey, familiar with the vine' and devoid of snakes. Bede knew Ireland as the great source of teaching for countless English monks — the brother of his own abbot Ceolfrith among them — and the inspiration for the ornate calligraphy of the Lindisfarne Gospels.

Let us then begin his great history where Bede began, with his survey of the land and peoples of 'an island in the Ocean' from his monastery on the Tyneside of thirteen centuries ago.

✛

THE SITUATION OF BRITAIN AND IRELAND
AND THEIR EARLIEST INHABITANTS

Britain is an island in the Ocean, and was once called Albion. It lies towards the north west, and faces Germany, Gaul and Spain, the largest areas of Europe, though at a considerable distance from them. From south to north it is 800 miles long, and its breadth is 200 miles, except for several promontories which extend further. If these are included, the complete coastline measures 4,875 miles. To the south lies Belgic Gaul, and the nearest harbour for travellers making the crossing is the city named Rutubi Portus, now known to the English in the corrupt form Reptacaestir. From here the distance across the sea to Gessoriacum in the land of the Morini, the nearest point on the coast of Gaul, is 50 miles, or, according to some authors, 450 stades. On the far side of Britain, where it lies open to the boundless Ocean, are the Orkney Islands.

The island is rich in crops and trees, and has good grazing for cattle and draught animals; it also produces vines in some areas. Land and sea birds, too, of various species flourish there, and it is famous for its rivers, with their abundance of fish, the salmon

Ecclesiastical History of the English People Book I Chapter 1

'They constructed a strong wall of stone in a straight line from sea to sea ... a famous landmark to this day'

Hadrian's Wall to the west of Housesteads.

and the eel in particular, and for its plentiful springs. Seals, dolphins and even whales are often caught, but most frequently of all various kinds of shellfish, including mussels in which excellent pearls of every colour — red, purple, violet, blue, green and, most common, white — are often found enclosed. There is a great abundance of whelks, from which a scarlet dye is derived whose glorious red colour can never be faded by the heat of the sun or damaged by the rain; indeed, the older it is, the lovelier it is. There are salt springs, and also hot springs, and the streams which flow from these provide hot baths for people of both sexes and every age, separately situated and adapted to their several needs. For water, as St Basil says, acquires the property of heat when it runs through metallic ores of certain kinds, and becomes not just hot but even scalding. Britain also has rich veins of metal — copper, iron, lead and silver — and produces a wealth of jet of the highest quality. This is a glossy black stone which burns when placed in the fire; when kindled, it drives away snakes, and, like amber, when warmed by rubbing it holds fast objects placed against it. The country was also once distinguished by twenty-eight of the finest cities, as well as countless fortresses, themselves strongly defended by walls, towers and barred gates.

Because Britain lies almost beneath the North Pole, its nights are light in the summer, so that often people watching at midnight are uncertain whether the evening twilight still lingers or morning dawn has already arrived. The reason is that during the night the sun returns to the east through the regions of the north and travels only a short distance below the horizon; and this also explains why the days are extremely long in the summer. On the other hand, the nights are extremely long in winter, eighteen hours in fact, no doubt because the sun at that time withdraws to African regions. Similarly, the nights in summer and the days in winter are very short, their length being only six equinoctial hours; whereas in Armenia, Macedonia, Italy and all other lands of the same latitude the longest day or night lasts fifteen hours and the shortest nine hours.

At the present time, corresponding to the number of the books containing the divine law, Britain uses the languages of five peoples to study and profess the one undivided knowledge of the supreme truth and true sublimity. These five are the languages of the English, the Britons, the Irish, the Picts, and the Latin language, the last of which through the reading of the scriptures is in general use among them all.

Originally this island was inhabited solely by Britons, from whom it took its name. They sailed to Britain, it is said, from the land of Armorica, and laid claim to the southern part of it.

After they had taken possession of most of the island, spreading from the south, it came about that the Picts from Scythia, so the story goes, sailed into the Ocean with a few warships and were driven by the wind beyond the furthest boundaries of Britain till they reached Ireland, where they landed on the north coast. Finding the Irish there they asked permission to make their own home in part of that land, but their request was refused. Now Ireland is the largest of all the islands after Britain, and lies to the west of Britain; but while shorter to the north, to the south it extends far beyond the limits of Britain and reaches as far as the north of Spain, though across a wide expanse of sea. It was to this land, then, that the Picts came on their voyage, as we have said, and asked that they too might be given a place there to make their home. The Irish replied that the island was not large enough for both peoples, but said: 'We can give you sound advice on what you can do. We know that there is another island not far from ours towards the east, and often on clearer days we can see it in the distance. If you will go there, you can make it your home; and if you meet with any resistance, make use of our help.' So the Picts made for Britain and began to settle in the northern part of the island, because the Britons had occupied the south. The Picts asked the Irish for wives, having none of their own, and they agreed only on condition that whenever the succession was in doubt they should choose their king from the female royal line rather than the male. This custom has been observed among the Picts to the present day, as is well known.

As time passed, Britain received a third people, the Irish, in addition to the Britons and the Picts, and they settled in the territory occupied by the Picts. They left Ireland under the leadership of Reuda, and either by treaty or by the sword claimed lands among the Picts which are their home to the present day. It is after that leader that they are still known as the Dalreudini, because in their language 'daal' means a part.

Ireland has a much more favourable latitude than Britain and enjoys a much healthier and milder climate. Snow seldom lies there more than three days, and no one cuts hay for winter during the summertime or builds stalls for the draught animals. No reptile is to be seen there, and no snake can live there; for although snakes have often been taken there from Britain, as the boat approaches the land they are affected by the scent of its air, and perish. In fact almost everything that comes from that island gives protection against poison. For example, when people were suffering from snake-bite we have seen the leaves of manu-scripts from Ireland scraped and the scrapings dropped in water and given as a drink; and this treatment immediately took away all the pain of the spreading poison and completely reduced the swelling. It is an island rich in milk and honey, familiar with the vine, and with plenty of fish and birds, and noted also for the hunting of the stag and the roe deer. Properly speaking, it is the native land of the Irish, and it was after leaving Ireland, as we have said, that they joined the Britons and the Picts as the third people of Britain.

There is a very long inlet from the sea, which was the ancient boundary between the Britons and the Picts, running inland from the west a great distance, and on it there is a city of the Britons called Alcluith, most strongly fortified to this day. It was to the north of this inlet that the Irish we have mentioned came and made their homeland.

The Roman Walls in the North

Bede follows his geographical prelude with an account of the Roman invasion and conquest of Britain, drawing on the writings of Orosius, a Spanish priest of the early sixth century from Tarragona, and adding material probably derived from his own contacts in Augustine's foundation at Canterbury.

Bede was writing only three centuries after the Roman legions left and the landscape he knew was dominated by the remains of their fortifications, while Roman roads were the thoroughfares for the battle-bound war-bands rampaging through the dawning of Saxon England. But it was the great Wall that would have stood as the Roman legacy most evident to Bede. Hadrian's Wall began its course of 73 miles 'from sea to sea' at Wallsend on the Tyne, just a few miles from Jarrow, and the Roman stones had their own importance to the Church of Bede's time. They served as the building blocks for the new monasteries, among them Benedict Biscop's dual foundation of St Peter and St Paul at Wearmouth and Jarrow.

When Bede came to write of the origins and history of the Roman walls in the north, he drew on the work of the British historian Gildas, writing in Latin in the sixth century, and added details of dimensions that he must have recorded from his own observations of the remaining fortifications. Thus Bede perpetuated Gildas' errors of chronology, dating the construction of both Hadrian's and Antoninus' walls some two and a half centuries too late.

But Bede's location of the walls is largely accurate, placing Hadrian's Wall between the Tyne and the Solway and Antoninus' earth-wall a hundred miles to the north, running from a point near Bo'ness on the Forth — close to the monastery of Abercorn that Bede called Aebbercurnig — to Alcluith, today's Dumbarton, on the Clyde.

Bede points to the great firths of Forth and Clyde as the natural frontiers of the Scottish tribes of Picts and Irish, indicating Alcluith in the west and Giudi in the east. Giudi is unknown on modern maps and, while it has been identified as either Inveresk or the isle of Inchkeith, it is possible that Bede was thinking of that natural outcrop where the Forth estuary becomes a river and Stirling Castle stands today.

Modern archaeology holds Bede's chronicle of the walls to be untenable. We can now date Hadrian's Wall to the decade following AD 120, and the raising of the Antonine Wall some twenty years later. Nonetheless, Bede's attempt to account for that vast complex of stone and earth fortifications — working from ancient texts and without maps — stood for eight and a half centuries as the only comprehensive theory of the Roman walls on Northumbria's northern frontier.

✢

SEVERUS RECOVERS PART OF BRITAIN AND DIVIDES IT FROM THE REST BY AN EARTHWORK

Ecclesiastical History of the English People Book I Chapter 5

In the year of our Lord 189, Severus, an African by birth from the town of Leptis in Tripolitania, became emperor. He was the seventeenth emperor after Augustus, and reigned for seventeen years. Harsh by nature, he was harassed throughout his reign by frequent wars, and governed the state with great courage, though beset by difficulties. Emerging victorious from the serious civil wars which had broken out during his reign, he was drawn to Britain by the desertion of nearly all the tribes there allied to Rome. In a series of great battles, keenly contested, he recovered part of the island, and decided that it should be marked off from the peoples who remained unconquered, not by a wall, as some suppose, but by an earthwork. For a wall is made of stones, whereas an earthwork, by which a camp is fortified to repel enemy attack, is made of sods of earth. After the sods are cut the earthwork is built up high above the ground like a wall, so that in front of it there is the ditch from which the sods have been lifted, and above the ditch stakes are fixed made of the toughest wood. So Severus built from sea to sea a great ditch and an earthwork of great strength, fortified and overlooked by towers at frequent intervals. While he was in Britain he fell ill and died at the town of Eboracum. He left two sons, Bassianus and Geta. Geta was judged an enemy of the state and put to death, while Bassianus took the surname Antoninus and became emperor.

✛

THE BRITONS ARE INVADED BY THE IRISH AND THE PICTS, AND ASK ROME
FOR MILITARY HELP; THE ROMANS RETURN AND BUILD A WALL ACROSS
THE ISLAND BUT THIS IS QUICKLY BREACHED BY THE SAME ENEMIES,
AND THE BRITONS ARE CRUSHED BY AN EVEN GREATER DISASTER

After this time the part of Britain inhabited by the Britons lay wholly exposed to the ravages of invaders. All their armed men, their entire military supplies, and the whole flower of their vigorous young warriors had been taken away by the reckless adventures of despots, never to return; and the people had no knowledge of the skills of warfare. As a result they suffered a sudden invasion from two warlike peoples across the sea, the Irish from the north-west and the Picts from the north, and their helpless plight continued for many years. We describe these people as living across the sea not because their homes lay outside Britain, but because they were separated from the territory of the Britons by two broad inlets from the sea which cut deep into Britain from its east and west coasts, though without meeting each other. The eastern inlet has halfway along it the town of Giudi; the western has above it, that is to say on its right bank, the town of Alcluith, which in their language means 'the rock of Clyde,' the name of the nearby river.

Ecclesiastical History of the English People Book I Chapter 12

Plagued by these peoples, the Britons sent messengers to Rome with letters bearing their tearful entreaties for help and their promise of permanent subjection to Rome if the enemy that oppressed them should be repelled. An armed legion was quickly assigned to them, sailed to the island, engaged with the enemy, and inflicted great losses on them, driving the survivors out of their allies' territory. Having freed the Britons for the moment from this cruel oppression, they urged them to build a defensive wall across the island from sea to sea to keep out the enemy; and the legion then returned home in great triumph. However, the islanders had no one with the expertise to carry out so ambitious a project, and built the wall demanded of them not of stone but of earth, so that it served no purpose. They built many miles of it between the two straits or inlets of the sea which we have mentioned, so that where the waters provided no defence they could protect their lands from enemy invasion by the earthwork. Perfectly clear remains of the work they constructed there, an earthwork of great breadth and height, can be seen even today. It starts about two miles to the west of the monastery of Aebbercurnig, at a place called Peanfahel in the Pictish language but in English Penneltun; and it stretches westwards to its furthest point near the town of Alcluith.

But when their former enemies saw that the Roman forces had left, they soon arrived again in their ships and invaded their borders, cutting down and trampling on everything that met their advance, like reapers mowing ripe corn. Again, therefore, messengers were sent to Rome with plaintive appeals for help. They begged them not to abandon their unhappy country to total destruction, and not to let the name of a Roman province, which for so long had shone brightly among them, be buried in disgrace by the lawless aggression of foreign nations. Again a legion was sent, and arriving unexpectedly in the autumn slaughtered large numbers of the enemy. Those who escaped were put to flight across those same waters over which in times past they had been driving their plunder each year without resistance.

This time the Romans put it to the Britons that they could no longer exhaust themselves with such testing campaigns in their defence. They urged them instead to take up arms themselves and make an effort to rival their enemies, who could only prevail over them if they were weakened by their own inaction. More than that, with the purpose of giving some further help to allies they were forced to abandon, they constructed a strong wall of stone in a straight line from sea to sea between the fortresses that had been built there for fear of the enemy, and where Severus had once built his earthwork. This wall, a famous landmark to this day, was built at public and private expense with the help of a contingent of Britons. It is eight feet wide and twelve feet high, and runs in a straight line from east to west, as can be clearly seen today. When it was built, the Romans lost no time in encouraging the dispirited people and instructing them in the manufacture of weapons. In addition, they built look-out towers at intervals on the shore of the Ocean to the south, where their ships lay, because there was fear of barbarian invasion from this direction also. They then said farewell to their allies, intending never to return again.

When they left for home, the Irish and the Picts, knowing that they did not mean to return, at once returned themselves, bolder than ever, and seized all the northernmost part of the island as far as the wall, as if it belonged to them. Stationed there on top of the defence was a dispirited and unnerved garrison, which languished by night and day in a state of terror; while the enemy for their part attacked unremittingly with hooked weapons. The cowardly defenders were dragged pitifully from the walls and dashed to the ground. In short, they abandoned their cities and the wall, and scattered. The enemy gave chase, and there followed a slaughter more cruel than any before it. Like lambs by wild beasts, so were the unhappy people torn to pieces by the enemy.

Alban, Protomartyr of Britain

In the course of the chapters on Roman Britain in Book I of the *Historia* we reach the point where Bede the hagiographer comes first and fully into his own. That point is his vivid account of the martyrdom of a citizen of Verulamium, who gave shelter to a Christian priest in a time of persecution, entered into the faith and then suffered death by beheading in the priest's stead.

The citizen's name was Alban and Bede's chronicle has remained until modern times as the authoritative history of England's first Christian martyr.

Bede, probably drawing on the early sixth-century *Passio Albani,* offers a story characteristically rich in the miraculous and wonderfully told. In both the *Historia* and the calendar of saints which he compiled at much the same time, Bede sets the date of Alban's martyrdom as 22 June, and so it remains in the Church calendar to this day. The year, however, has come into question as modern historians cast doubt on Bede — following Gildas — setting Alban's story in the time of the Diocletian persecution of Christians in the first years of the fourth century. It seems now that Alban may have suffered under the persecution of Septimius Severus a full century earlier — as the sixth-century text suggests — but today's official records admit that Alban's date is effectively unknown.

Medieval historians have made much of Offa of Mercia's endowment of the church on the site of Alban's martyrdom, but Bede records the existence of a fine church there in his own time, some fifty years before Offa. It was, according to Bede, the site of numerous miraculous cures for pilgrims at the martyr's shrine, so we may imagine an imposing and wealthy foundation that was to become even richer through the generosity of the great Mercian king.

Bede records Alban's home as Verulamium, 'which the English ... call Verlamacaestir or Vaeclingacaestir.' It was long after Bede's time that the city adopted the name of its saint to become St Albans in modern Hertfordshire. There stands the great Norman cathedral and abbey church, built of Roman brick from the ruins of Verulamium, on the traditional site of the martyrdom and enclosing within its walls the shrine of the proto-martyr of Britain.

'A church was built there, whose magnificent workmanship made it a fitting memorial to Alban's martyrdom'

The Cathedral and Abbey Church of St Alban — built on the traditional site of his martyrdom — seen through the ruined Roman wall of Verulamium.

✢

THE MARTYRDOM OF SAINT ALBAN AND HIS COMPANIONS, WHO AT THAT TIME SHED THEIR BLOOD ON THE LORD'S BEHALF

Ecclesiastical History of the English People Book I Chapter 7

During this persecution there occurred the martyrdom of St Alban. The priest Fortunatus in his 'Praise of the Virgins,' when mentioning the blessed martyrs who came to the Lord from every part of the world, says this of him:

'Illustrious Alban fruitful Britain bore.'

It was this Alban, who, though still a pagan, at the time when heathen emperors were issuing savage edicts against the Christians, gave hospitality to a priest who was in flight from his persecutors. Alban noticed that he devoted himself day and night to continual prayer and vigil, and suddenly he himself received the gift of divine grace and began to imitate the example of his faith and piety. Gradually, instructed and encouraged by him in the way of salvation, he abandoned the darkness of idolatry and became a whole-hearted Christian. After this priest had been staying as his guest for several days, it came to the ears of the wicked ruler that one who confessed the Christian faith — but who was not yet destined for martyrdom — was hiding at Alban's home. He at once ordered his soldiers to make a thorough search for him there. When they arrived at the martyr's humble dwelling, St Alban at once offered himself to the soldiers in place of his guest and teacher, wearing the clothing, that is to say the cloak, worn by the priest. He was bound and taken before a judge.

Now it happened that, at the time when Alban was being brought to him, the judge was officiating at the altars of evil spirits and offering sacrifices to them. Seeing Alban, he at once flared up in anger that he had presumed of his own choice to offer himself to the soldiers, and put his life at risk, in place of the guest he had harboured. He ordered him to be dragged before the idols of the evil spirits where he was standing, and said: 'Because you chose to conceal a sacrilegious rebel, rather than hand him over to the soldiers to pay the penalty he deserved for his blasphemy and contempt of the gods, you must suffer all the punishments that were due to him, if you attempt to forsake our worship and religion.' But St Alban, who had freely admitted his Christian allegiance to the persecutors of the faith, had no fear of the ruler's threats: clad in the armour of spiritual warfare, he openly declared his refusal to obey his orders. The judge then asked: 'What is your family and race?' Alban replied: 'What concern of yours is it to know my parentage? But if you wish to hear the truth about my religion, you must know that I am now a Christian and ready to perform the duties of a Christian.' The judge said: 'I want to know your name: tell me it at once.' He answered: 'I am called Alban by my parents, and I adore and worship forever the true and living God, who created all things.' At this point the judge, overcome with anger, said: 'If you wish to enjoy the happiness of eternal life, make sacrifice to the great gods without delay.' Alban replied: 'These sacrifices, which you offer to evil spirits, can give no help to their worshippers nor fulfil the desires and prayers of their suppliants. The truth is rather that anyone who has offered sacrifices to these idols will receive as his reward the everlasting torments of Hell.'

Hearing this, the judge was enraged and ordered God's holy confessor to be beaten by the torturers, supposing that his resolution of heart, on which words had no effect, could be weakened by wounds. Yet in spite of suffering the keenest tortures, Alban bore them with patience, in fact with joy, for the Lord's sake. When the judge realized that he could not be broken by torture nor turned back from the worship of the Christian religion, he ordered him to be beheaded.

As he was being taken to his death, he came to a fast flowing river, which separated the city wall and the arena where he was to be executed; and he saw there a large crowd of men and women of every age and rank, who without doubt were summoned by divine inspiration to escort the most blessed confessor and martyr. They filled the bridge over the river itself in such numbers that he could hardly have crossed that evening. In fact almost everyone had gone out, and the judge was left in the city without an escort. So St Alban, whose burning desire was to come quickly to his martyrdom, approached the torrent, and as he lifted his eyes to Heaven, suddenly the river bed became dry and he saw that the water had receded and made a way for him to walk. Among those who saw this happen was the very executioner who was to behead him, and when Alban reached the spot appointed for his death, he hurried to meet him, acting surely on divine prompting. He threw down the sword which he held ready drawn, and prostrated himself at his feet, longing to be himself judged worthy of execution, together with, or instead of, the martyr whom he was commanded to execute.

So while he was converted from a persecutor to a companion in the true faith, and the executioners stayed their hand, as was right, while the sword lay on the ground, God's most reverend confessor climbed a hill accompanied by the crowd. The hill, about five hundred paces from the arena, was, as was fitting, a joyous and lovely sight, clothed all over as it was with the varied colours of wild flowers; nowhere was it steep or precipitous or sheer, but nature made its broad sides slope gently down into a flat plain, rendering it by its intrinsic beauty from of old a fit place to be hallowed by the blood of a blessed martyr.

On top of the hill St Alban asked God for a gift of water, and at once a perpetual spring gushed up at his feet, channelled into a stream, to prove to them all that even the torrent had rendered service to the martyr. For it was not possible that the martyr would ask for water on the hill top after leaving the river bed dry, unless he had known it to be at hand. The river, its service performed and its sacred duty fulfilled, returned to its natural course, leaving testimony of its obedience. And so the brave martyr was beheaded on that spot and received the crown of life that God has promised to those that love Him. But the man who laid unholy hands upon his holy neck was not permitted to gloat over his body: his eyes dropped to the ground together with the blessed martyr's head.

Also beheaded there was the soldier who earlier, constrained by Heaven's will, refused to strike God's holy confessor; and there can be no doubt that although he was not purified by the water of baptism, yet he was washed clean by his own blood and made worthy to enter the Kingdom of Heaven. After this the judge, alarmed by the strange and heaven-sent miracles, ordered an immediate end to the persecution, and began to respect the deaths of the martyrs, which previously he had thought to be the means of destroying their commitment to the Christian faith. St Alban was martyred on the twenty-second of June near the city of Verulamium, which the English today call Verlamacaestir or Vaeclingacaestir. In later times, with the return of the peace of Christianity, a church was built there, whose magnificent workmanship made it a fitting memorial to Alban's martyrdom; and to this very day it has continued to win renown for the healing of the sick and the frequent working of miracles.

'With the Ebb and Flow of the Tide ...'

Oswald and Aidan

The great age of Northumbria, in which Bede himself figures so prominently, dawned on a morning in the fourth decade of the seventh century when Oswald — soon to stand as one of the seven *Bretwaldas* listed in the *Historia* — raised a wooden cross as his battle standard on the Roman Wall not far from Hexham.

Bede offers a succinct chronicle of the long years of the sword that saw the settlement of Saxon England and the emergence of the two royal houses which ruled Anglo-Saxon Northumbria. In the south — in what later became Yorkshire — lay the kingdom of Deira. The name derives from the British word *deifre*, 'waters,' suggesting its origin on the banks of the Humber. Aelle, son of the earliest recorded Deiran king Yffi, was conquered by the rising power of Bernicia late in the sixth century.

The house of Bernicia began with the Saxon warlord Ida — probably commanding no more than a few dozen men in a handful of ships — who laid claim to that outcrop of the Great Whin Sill known today as Bamburgh. There he raised his fortress and from there his dynasty of Bernicia dominated Northumbrian history until Bede's time.

Bamburgh — its name deriving from Bebba, one of the first of the queens of Bernicia — was the base from which Aethelric ventured out to conquer Aelle and unite Northumbria under a single overlord. Aethelric's son, Aethelfrith, took up his father's sword as befitted a pagan warlord claiming ancestry back through Baeldaeg to Woden himself.

In 603 Aethelfrith defeated the Scots on the field of Degsastan and went on to crush the British at Chester. Turning his ambitions southwards in 616, he met with fierce resistance. Aelle's son Edwin — in alliance with Raedwald of East Anglia — joined battle with Aethelfrith on the river Idle and restored ascendancy to Deira.

Raedwald, numbered by Bede among the *Bretwaldas*, has achieved his own immortality, in the richly endowed ship-burial at Sutton Hoo. This, it now seems, according to the latest archaeological research, is the magnificent legacy of Raedwald's funeral.

Meanwhile, Aethelfrith's sons fled north to safety, amongst them the young Oswald destined to return sword in hand before two decades were past. Bede's account of Edwin's reign tells of a time when a mother carrying her newborn child could walk in safety across the breadth of the land. If this were so, it was very probably because the kingdom was governed by a warlord of similar stature to a Roman emperor in centuries past, and Bede's generous regard for Edwin was surely inspired by his importance as the first *Bretwalda* to rule as a Christian king.

Christianity had established its first firm footholds on the mainland in the second half of the sixth century. First came Columba, travelling over the sea from Ireland to settle on the isle of Iona — known to Bede as Hii — from where he carried his faith into the hills and glens of the western highlands and islands.

In the last decade of the sixth century, Augustine arrived in Kent, establishing his church at Canterbury and converting the Saxon overlords of the southern kingdoms.

When Edwin took the Kentish princess Aethelberga as his queen, she travelled north with Augustine's priest Paulinus in her company, and to Paulinus fell the task of converting the Northumbrian king to the faith. It was a task that took some time, but eventually, on Easter Day in the year 627, Edwin was baptized in a Saxon church raised amid the Roman stones of Eboracum. His reign as a Christian king was to last little over half a decade. By 633, enemies were gathering and a host led by Cadwalla of Gwynedd and Penda of Mercia slew Edwin in battle at Haethfelth — known today as Hatfield. A reign of terror was unleashed on the north country as Edwin's kingdom was mercilessly ravaged by his vengeful conquerors.

His queen fled home to Kent and with her went the priest Paulinus, leaving many of those he had converted to revert to their pagan practices. Edwin's Northumbria crumbled once more into the two kingdoms of Deira and Bernicia ruled by the sons of Aethelfrith and Edwin until they too fell to the swords of Penda and Cadwalla.

And so, from his sanctuary on Columba's Iona came Oswald, the second son of Aethelfrith, to claim the kingdom that his father had forged. From the fortress at Bamburgh he marched to muster his army in the North Tyne valley. Cadwalla was also on the march, leading his battle horde up the old Roman Dere Street to Hexham — known to Bede as Hagustaldesea.

On the night before the armies clashed across the old Roman wall — according to Adamnan of Iona — Oswald had a vision of Columba. The next morning he confronted the enemy who had destroyed Edwin and ravaged Northumbria. The conflict was savage and wide-ranging. Skulls and swordblades have been found in the fields that fall away to the south of Oswald's line of battle. The men of Gwynedd made their last stand some five miles to the north and Cadwalla himself is said to have been slain three miles to the south of Hexham at Rowley Burn, the stream that Bede calls Denisesburn.

Oswald returned to Bamburgh in triumph, to unite Northumbria under the royal house of Bernicia and look to his childhood sanctuary of Iona for a priest who would restore Christianity to his kingdom. He brought Aidan from Iona to found a monastery on the tidal island of Lindisfarne, so well sited in Celtic monastic tradition and yet within sight of Oswald's fortress of Bamburgh.

The golden age of Northumbrian Christianity was dawning. Ahead lay the great centuries of art and learning on Lindisfarne, the splendid foundation of Wearmouth and Jarrow, and the great dispute at Whitby as to whether the northern church should offer allegiance to Iona or to Rome.

The first light of that dawn came on a morning in the year 634 — according to Bede, a year later or earlier according to others — when battle was joined under the shadow of the cross at a place known as Heaven's Field.

✝

THE IMMEDIATE SUCCESSORS OF KING EDWIN ABANDON
THE FAITH OF THEIR PEOPLE, AND OSWALD, A MOST CHRISTIAN KING,
RESTORES BOTH KINGDOMS

Ecclesiastical History of the English People Book III Chapter 1

After Edwin's death in battle, the throne of Deira, the kingdom to which his ancestors had belonged and where his reign had begun, passed to a son of his uncle Aelfric; his name was Osric, and he had received the mysteries of the Christian faith during the mission of Paulinus. But the kingdom of Bernicia, the other ancient division of Northumbria, passed to Eanfrith, son of Aethelfrith, who claimed descent from its royal family. Throughout Edwin's reign the sons of this Aethelfrith, his predecessor, were living in exile with a large company of young nobles among the Irish and the Picts, and while there they were instructed in the faith as taught by the Irish and regenerated by the grace of baptism. On the death of their enemy the king they were allowed to return to their own country, and the eldest of them, Eanfrith, as we have mentioned, became king of Bernicia.

'Illustrious Alban fruitful Britain bore'

St Alban's shrine in the Cathedral and Abbey Church of St Alban.

Both of these kings no sooner gained the crown of their earthly kingdom than they forswore and betrayed the mysteries of the Kingdom of Heaven into which they had been initiated, and surrendered themselves again to defilement and destruction in the filthy practice of idolatry.

Before long both were slain by Cadwalla, king of the Britons, and met their just retribution at the hand of a heathen. First, the following summer he killed Osric, who had rashly laid siege to him in a fortified town. Cadwalla suddenly broke out with all his men, caught Osric unprepared, and destroyed him and his entire army. He then occupied the Northumbrian kingdoms for a whole year, not like a victorious king assuming ownership but like a cruel tyrant ravaging and tearing them apart with dreadful loss of life. Finally, when Eanfrith imprudently came to sue for peace with an escort of only twelve thanes, he visited the same fate upon him. Even today that remains an ill-omened year and hateful to all good people, both because of the apostasy of the English kings who cast aside the mysteries of the faith, and because of the savage tyranny of the king of the Britons. Consequently all those who calculate the dates of the kings have agreed to expunge the memory of the apostate kings and to assign that year to the reign of their successor, Oswald, a man beloved of God. After the murder of his brother Eanfrith Oswald arrived with an army small in numbers but protected by their faith in Christ, and he slew the accursed leader of the Britons and all that vast army that he boasted none could resist, at a place called in English Denisesburn, meaning the stream of Denise.

✢

COUNTLESS MIRACLES OF HEALING ARE WROUGHT
BY THE WOOD OF THE CROSS WHICH OSWALD HAD SET UP
ON GOING INTO BATTLE AGAINST THE HEATHEN

Ecclesiastical History of the English People Book III Chapter 2 On approaching this battle Oswald set up the sign of the holy cross and on bended knees besought God to send heavenly succour to his worshippers in the hour of their need; and the place is pointed out to this day and held in great reverence. Indeed it is said that when the cross had been quickly made and a hole made ready for it to stand in, Oswald himself, fired by his faith, seized it and placed it in its hole and held it upright with both hands, until the soldiers heaped up the soil and made it fast in the ground. Thereupon he raised his voice and cried aloud to the whole army: 'Let us all kneel, and together pray the almighty, everliving and true God to defend us by His mercy from a proud and cruel enemy; for He knows that the war we have engaged in for the deliverance of our people is a just war.' They all did as he had ordered and, advancing thus against the enemy as dawn appeared, won the victory as the reward for their faith. At the place where they prayed countless miracles of healing are known to have been wrought, a sure proof and memorial of the king's faith. To this day many visitors cut off splinters of wood from the holy cross and put them in water, which they either give to drink or sprinkle upon sick people or beasts; and these are quickly restored to health.

The place is called in English Hefenfelth, meaning Heaven's Field, a name given it in ancient times in evident anticipation of what was to come; for it signified that Heaven's standard was to be set up there, Heaven's victory won, and Heaven's miracles to continue unceasing to the present time. It lies to the north near the wall with which the Romans, as we have described earlier, encompassed the whole of Britain from sea to sea to protect it against barbarian attacks. It was in this place that the brothers of the nearby church of Hagustaldesea long ago established the custom of gathering each year on the eve of the anniversary of King Oswald's death and holding a vigil for the salvation of his soul; and on the following morning they would sing many psalms of praise and offer the holy sacrifice and oblation on his behalf. As the fame of this good custom has spread, they have lately built a church on the site and made the place more sacred and esteemed than any other in the eyes of all men. This is as it should be, for as far as we know there was no symbol of the Christian faith, no church, and no altar erected anywhere in the land of Bernicia until their new leader in war, inspired by his zeal for the faith, set up this standard of the holy cross before doing battle with his monstrous enemy.

'The royal town named after the former queen Bebba'

The great fortress crag of Bamburgh from the shore of Lindisfarne. On this rock in the year 547, Ida established *Bebbanburg* as the royal capital of the Anglo-Saxon kingdom of Northumbria.

It is not out of place to describe one of the many miracles that have been performed at this cross. A few years ago, one of the brothers of the church of Hagustaldesea, named Bothelm, who is still alive, was walking at night on the ice without proper care and suddenly fell and broke his arm. The fracture caused him great distress, as the pain prevented him even from moving his arm towards his mouth. Hearing one day that one of the brothers had arranged to go up to the site of the holy cross, he asked him to bring him on his return a piece of the venerable wood, telling him that he believed this could be the means of his recovery, if the Lord granted it. The other did as he was asked and, returning in the evening when the brothers were now seated at dinner, he presented him with a piece of the ancient moss which covered the surface of the wood. Bothelm was sitting at the table and had nothing to hand in which to keep safe the proffered gift, and so he put it in his habit; and when he went to bed he forgot to take it out and allowed it to stay there. Waking up in the middle of the night he felt something cold lying by his side, and when he moved his hand to find what it was he discovered that his arm and hand were as sound as if they had never pained him.

✝

KING OSWALD ASKS THE IRISH FOR A BISHOP AND AIDAN IS SENT TO HIM;
HE GIVES AIDAN AN EPISCOPAL SEE ON THE ISLAND OF LINDISFARNE

Ecclesiastical History of the English People
Book III
Chapter 3

As soon as Oswald came to the throne, he was anxious that all the people under his rule should be filled with the grace of the Christian faith, whose power he had experienced to the full in his victory over the heathen. So he sent to the Irish elders, from whom he and his escort had received the sacrament of baptism when in exile, and asked them to send him a bishop, by whose teaching and ministry the English people that he ruled might learn the blessings of faith in the Lord and receive the sacraments. He obtained his request without delay, and was sent Bishop Aidan, a man of great gentleness, holiness and moderation, who had a zeal for God, though not wholly in accordance

with knowledge. In the fashion of his people, which we have often referred to, he used to observe Easter Sunday between the fourteenth and the twentieth day of the moon. The northern province of the Irish and the whole nation of the Picts were still celebrating Easter in that style, believing that they followed in that observance the writings of Anatolius, a holy and respected father of the Church. The truth of this anyone with knowledge will determine without difficulty. But the Irish peoples who lived in the southern parts of Ireland learned long before to observe Easter according to canonical custom, in obedience to the ruling of the bishop of the Apostolic See.

When the bishop arrived, the king granted him the island of Lindisfarne, as he requested, to be his episcopal see. With the ebb and flow of the tide, this is a place that is twice a day encircled by the waves of the sea, like an island, and twice rejoined to the mainland when its shore becomes exposed again. In all matters Oswald listened humbly and joyfully to the bishop's advice, and showed great concern to build up and extend the Church of Christ within his kingdom. The bishop was not fully conversant with the English language, and on many occasions it was delightful to watch while he preached the gospel, and the king himself, having acquired a perfect knowledge of Irish during his long exile, acted as interpreter of Heaven's word for his aldermen and thanes.

From that time many missionaries from Irish territory began to arrive in Britain as the days went by, who preached the word of the faith with great zeal to the English kingdoms ruled over by Oswald; and to those who believed, such of them as held the rank of priest administered the grace of baptism. Churches were built in various places, and the people gladly flocked together to hear the Word. By the gift of the king estates and lands were granted for the establishment of monasteries, and English boys together with their elders were given systematic instruction by Irish teachers and taught to observe the discipline of a Rule.

For those who came to preach were mostly monks. Bishop Aidan himself was a monk; he was sent from the island of Hii, whose monastery was for a long time chief among most of the northern Irish and all the Picts, exercising control over their peoples. This island belongs to Britain, being separated from it by a narrow strait, but was long ago given to Irish monks by the Picts who inhabit that part of Britain, because it was through the monks' preaching that they adopted the Christian faith.

✝

THE PICTS RECEIVE THE CHRISTIAN FAITH

In the year of our Lord 565, when Justin the Younger succeeded Justinianus as ruler of the Roman Empire, there came to Britain from Ireland a priest and abbot named Columba, a true monk in his life as in his habit, to preach the word of God to the kingdoms of the northern Picts; these people are separated from the southern territories of the Picts by a range of steep and rugged mountains. The southern Picts themselves, whose homes are on this side of these mountains, are said to have given up the errors of idolatry long before this and received the true faith through the preaching of the word by Bishop Ninian, a most reverend and holy man of British race, who had received orthodox instruction at Rome in the mysteries of the true faith. His episcopal see, distinguished by its church dedicated to St Martin, where his body rests together with many other saints, is now under the rule of the English. The place is part of the kingdom of Bernicia and popularly known as the White House, because Ninian built a church of stone there, a style of building unfamiliar to the Britons.

Ecclesiastical History of the English People Book III Chapter 4

Now Columba came to Britain in the ninth year of the reign of Bruide, son of Maelchon, a Pictish king of great power, and converted the people to the Christian faith by his word and his example; and because of this they gave him possession of the island mentioned above to build a monastery. It is a small island, about five hides in area according to English reckoning, and his successors live there to this day. Columba himself was buried there, having died at the age of seventy-seven about thirty-two years after coming to preach in Britain. Before coming to Britain he had built a noble monastery in Ireland, called

Dearmach in the Irish language, meaning the field of the oaks, after the many oak trees that stand there. His disciples from both of these monasteries went on to found many more monasteries in Britain and in Ireland, over all of which the island monastery, where his body lies at rest, held pre-eminence.

The island itself always has as its ruler an abbot in priest's orders, to whose jurisdiction the whole province, including even the bishops, is subject. This unusual arrangement follows the precedent of their first teacher, who was not a bishop but a priest and a monk. It is said that his disciples possess some written records of his life and teaching, but whatever type of man he may have been, we know for certain that he left to succeed him men distinguished by great abstinence, a love of God, and observance of the Rule. It is true that they followed unreliable calculations of the date of the greatest Christian festival, as they lived at the far ends of the earth and no one had acquainted them with the synodal decrees about the observance of Easter; but they diligently practised those works of devotion and purity which they could learn from the writings of the prophets, evangelists and apostles. They persisted in this reckoning of the date of Easter for a considerable time, a hundred and fifty years in fact, until the year of our Lord 715.

In that year, however, they were visited by Egbert, of English race, a most reverend and holy father and bishop, who had for long been an exile in Ireland for the sake of Christ, and was most learned in the scriptures and famed for his long and saintly life; and they were set right by him and converted to the true and canonical date of Easter. Previously, they did not always follow the Jewish practice, as some supposed, and observe it on the fourteenth day of the moon; they always observed Easter on a Sunday, but in the wrong week. As Christians they knew that the resurrection of the Lord, which occurred on the day after the Sabbath, must always be celebrated on the day after the Sabbath; but being an uncivilized and ignorant people they had never learned when that first day after the Sabbath, now called the Lord's Day, should occur. Even so, because the grace of Christian love never failed to inspire them, they were accounted worthy of full knowledge of this matter also, in accordance with

'On approaching this battle Oswald set up the sign of the holy cross ... and the place is pointed out to this day and held in great reverence'

The battlefield of *Hefenfelth* at Chollerford, Northumberland. The church in the background stands on the site where Oswald raised his standard, while the modern cross stands on his line of battle along the vallum of the Wall.

the promise of the apostle when he says: 'And if in anything ye be otherwise minded, God shall reveal even this unto you.' We shall have more to say on this subject in its proper place in the pages that follow.

✛

THE LIFE OF BISHOP AIDAN

Ecclesiastical History of the English People Book III Chapter 5

It was from this island, then, and this community of monks that Aidan was sent after his consecration as bishop to instruct the English kingdom in the faith of Christ, at the time when Seghine, abbot and priest, was in charge of the monastery. Among the lessons that Aidan had given the clergy about the conduct of their lives there was none more salutary than his own example of abstinence and self-discipline; and his teaching commended itself to everyone above all because he taught the way of life that he and his followers practised. He neither sought nor cared for the possessions of this world, and he took delight in giving away to poor people whom he met all the gifts he received from kings and rich men of the world. He used to travel everywhere, whether in town or in the country, not on horseback but on foot, unless forced to do otherwise by some urgent necessity, so that wherever as he walked he caught sight of people, rich or poor, he could at once turn and speak to them. If they were unbelievers he would invite them to accept the mystery of the faith; while those who already believed he would strengthen in the faith and encourage by his words and actions in the practice of almsgiving and works of mercy.

His way of life was in great contrast to the slothfulness of our own times, so much so that all who travelled with him, whether tonsured or laymen, were required to study, that is to occupy themselves in reading the scriptures or learning the psalms. This was the daily task of Aidan and all his company wherever they went. If it chanced, as it seldom did, that he was summoned to feast with the king, he attended with one or two of his clergy, and after a little refreshment made haste to leave to continue reading with his followers, or else to pray. Inspired by his ex-

ample many devout men and women at that time formed the
habit of prolonging their fast on Wednesday and Friday until the
ninth hour, except for the period between Easter and Pentecost.
If wealthy people did wrong he never kept silent out of deference or fear, but would correct them with a stern rebuke. He
never gave money to powerful men of the world, but only food
to such as he entertained; and those gifts of money that he
received from the rich he preferred to distribute for the use of
the poor, as we have said, or spend in ransoming people unjustly sold into slavery. In fact many of those he had ransomed
later became his disciples, and after training and instructing
them he ordained them to the priesthood.

It is said that when King Oswald asked the Irish for a
bishop to teach the faith to him and his people, another man
of sterner temperament was sent at first; but although he
preached among the English for some time he met with no
success, and the people were unwilling to listen to him. He
therefore returned home and announced at a meeting of the
elders that he had been able to make no headway in teaching
the nation to which he had been sent, for they were an in-
tractable people of stubborn and uncivilized character. They are
said to have held a long discussion at their conference on what
should be done, as they wished to bring to that people the
salvation they sought, while regretting that the preacher
they had sent had not been welcomed. Then Aidan, who was at
the meeting himself, said to the priest in question: 'It seems to
me, brother, that you have been unduly severe with your ignorant hearers. You should have followed the guidance of
the apostle and offered them at first the milk of simpler teaching, until gradually, growing strong on the food of God's word,
they could take in a fuller statement of the faith and carry out
God's more exalted commands.' When they heard this, everyone
present turned to look at Aidan, and after careful consideration
of the meaning of his words, they resolved that it was he who
should be made bishop and sent to instruct an unbelieving and
ignorant people, because he had proved himself to be endowed
above all with the grace of discretion, which is the mother of
all the virtues; and so they consecrated him and sent him to

preach. As time went on he showed himself to be blessed not only with that discretion and good sense but with the other virtues also.

✝

THE WONDERFUL DEVOTION AND PIETY OF KING OSWALD

Ecclesiastical
History of the
English People
Book III
Chapter 6

Such then was the bishop who gave instruction in the faith to King Oswald and the English nation that he ruled; and Oswald not only learned to hope for a kingdom in Heaven unknown to his ancestors, but also gained a greater earthly kingdom than any of his predecessors, from the same one God who made Heaven and earth. In fact he brought under his control all the peoples and kingdoms of Britain, speaking between them four different languages, British, Pictish, Irish and English.

Yet it is wonderful to relate of one elevated to such a height of kingly power, that he was always humble, kind and generous towards the poor and towards strangers. For example, it is said that once on Easter Day when he was sitting at dinner with the bishop, and a silver dish was placed before him on the table full of royal fare, they were about to raise their hands to ask a blessing on the bread when one of his officers, whose duty it was to bring relief to the needy, suddenly came in and told the king that a large crowd of poor people from every district was sitting in the precincts, asking for alms from the king. He at once ordered the meal that had been served to him to be taken out to the poor, and the dish to be broken in pieces and divided among them. When he saw it, the bishop who sat with him was delighted by the act of mercy, and took his right hand and said: 'May this hand never wither with age.' And his prayer and blessing were fulfilled, for when Oswald was killed in battle his hand and arm were severed from his body, and they remain undecayed to this day. They are preserved in the royal town named after Bebba a former queen, stored in a silver casket in the church of St Peter, and are venerated with due honour by everyone.

Through the efforts of this king the kingdoms of Deira and

Bernicia, which were previously at enmity with each other, were peacefully united and became one people. Oswald was the nephew of King Edwin through his sister Acha, and it was fitting that so great a predecessor should have such a kinsman to inherit both his religion and his throne.

✟

AT THE PLACE WHERE OSWALD WAS KILLED
MANY MIRACLES OF HEALING OCCUR

Oswald, that most Christian king of Northumbria, reigned for nine years, including that year which had been made an object of loathing by the unholy savagery of the king of the Britons and the insane apostasy of the English kings. For, as we have explained above, it was decided by general agreement that the name and memory of the apostates should be wholly expunged from the list of Christian kings, and no year assigned to their reign. At the end of this period Oswald was killed in a great battle against the same heathen people, the Mercians, and their heathen king, as had slain his predecessor Edwin. The date was the fifth of August, and he was thirty-eight years old. The place where he died is called in English Maserfelth.

Ecclesiastical History of the English People Book III Chapter 9

How great a faith he had in God, and what devotion of heart, was revealed even after his death by miracles. At the place where he was killed by the heathen when fighting for his country, to this day miraculous cures of sick people and animals continue to occur. It has often happened that people have taken away the very soil where his body fell to the ground and put it in water, and by its use have brought great relief to their sick. This practice became so common that the gradual removal of the earth made a trench as deep as a man's height. It is not surprising that the sick are healed at the spot where he died, when throughout his life he never ceased to care for the sick and the poor, to give them alms, and to bring them help. Many are the miracles that are related as being wrought at that spot or by the soil from that spot; but we consider it sufficient to mention only two, which we have heard from our elders.

Not long after Oswald's death, it happened that a man was travelling near the spot on horseback, when suddenly his horse grew weak, stopped and lowered its head to the ground, and then, foaming at the mouth and in increasing distress, fell to the earth. Its rider dismounted, removed the saddle, and waited to see whether the horse would recover or he would have to leave it dead. It was tormented by severe pain for a long time, twisting and turning in different directions, when suddenly it rolled on to the spot where the famous king fell dead. At once the pain ceased and the frantic writhing of its body was stilled; then, as horses do, it rolled from side to side as if it had been resting, and promptly stood up completely cured and began hungrily to crop the grass.

Seeing this and being a shrewd man, the traveller realized that the place where the horse was cured possessed some special sanctity, so he put up a sign there before mounting his horse and coming to the inn where he intended to stay. On his arrival he found a girl there, a niece of the patron, who had long been afflicted with paralysis; and when he heard members of the household speaking sadly of her cruel infirmity, he told them of the place where his horse had been cured. Without more ado they put her in a cart, took her to the place, and laid her down there. She fell asleep on the spot for a short time, and when she awoke found that she was healed of her disease. She then asked for water and washed her face; arranged her hair and put on a linen headscarf; and then, accompanied by those who had brought her, returned on foot and in good health.

✛

THE SOIL FROM THAT PLACE HAS POWER TO RESIST FIRE

Ecclesiastical History of the English People
Book III
Chapter 10

At the same time another traveller said to be of British race passed by the site where the battle took place, and noticed that one patch of ground was greener and more beautiful than the rest of the field. He made a shrewd guess that the reason why the grass was especially green at that spot must be that some man of more saintly character than the rest of the army had been killed there. So he took with him some soil from the ground there wrapped in linen cloth, thinking that the soil would serve to cure the sick; and events were to prove him right. Continuing on his journey he came to a village in the evening, and entered a house where the villagers were enjoying a feast; and he was welcomed by the owners of the house and joined them at the feast, hanging up the linen cloth with the soil he had brought on a wall post. The feasting and carousing were continuing long into the evening round a large blazing fire, when sparks flying up into the roof, which was made of wattles and thatched with hay, suddenly engulfed it in flames. As soon as the revellers realized this they rushed out in panic, unable to save the burning house, which was on the point of destruction. So the house was burned down, but the post alone, on which that bag of soil was hanging, remained safe and untouched by the fire. They were astonished to see this miracle, and by careful enquiry discovered that the soil had been taken from the place where King Oswald's blood had been spilt. The fame of these miracles spread far and wide, and as the days passed many people began to visit the place and obtain there the grace of healing for themselves and their families.

A HEAVENLY LIGHT STANDS ALL NIGHT OVER HIS RELICS,
AND DEMONIACS ARE CURED BY HIM

On the same topic we must on no account omit to mention the miracles and signs from Heaven that occurred when his bones were found and transferred to the church where they are now preserved. This was done through the efforts of Osthryth, queen of the Mercians, the daughter of his brother Oswy, who ruled the kingdom after him, as we shall describe later.

Ecclesiastical History of the English People Book III Chapter 11

In the kingdom of Lindsey there is a noble monastery called Beardaneu, for which this queen and her husband Aethelred felt a special love and reverence, and which they enriched with gifts; and she wanted to give her uncle's bones an honourable burial there. When the cart carrying the bones arrived at the monastery towards evening, the community were reluctant to receive them, because, though they knew Oswald to be a saint, he had come from another kingdom and had once conquered them; so they pursued him with their longstanding hatred even after his death, with the result that the relics stayed outside that night, with merely a large tent spread over the cart which carried them. But a miraculous sign from Heaven revealed with what reverence they ought to be received by all the faithful. All that night a pillar of light stood over the cart and stretched upwards to the sky, clearly visible in almost every part of the kingdom of Lindsey. When morning came, therefore, the brothers who the day before had refused to admit the relics of God's beloved saint, earnestly requested that they might be buried in their monastery. They washed the bones, put them in a casket prepared for their burial, and laid them in the church with due honour; and so that the king and saint should have a lasting memorial, they put over his tomb his banner of gold and purple, and the water in which they had washed his bones was poured away in a corner of the cemetery. Ever afterwards the earth which received the holy water had the power and saving grace of driving out devils from the bodies of people possessed.

Some time later, when Queen Osthryth was staying at the monastery, she was visited by a venerable abbess, still alive today, named Aethelhild, the sister of two saintly men, Aethelwin, bishop of Lindsey, and Aldwin, abbot of the monastery of Beardaneu. The abbess, whose own monastery was not far from Aldwin's, talked with the queen on her visit to Beardaneu, and when the conversation turned on Oswald said that she herself on that night had seen the light over his relics rising up to the sky. At this the queen mentioned that many sick people had already been cured by soil from the floor on which the water that had washed his bones had been poured. The abbess asked to be given some of the health giving soil, and taking it she wrapped it in a cloth, put it in a casket, and went back. Some time later when she was at her own monastery, a guest arrived there, who often during the hours of night used to suffer sudden and severe attacks by an unclean spirit. He was made welcome, and after dinner had lain down on his bed, when suddenly he was possessed by a devil and began to cry out, gnash his teeth, foam at the mouth, and twist his body convulsively. As no one could hold him or tie him down, a servant ran and knocked on the abbess's gate and reported what had happened. Opening the monastery door she went out with one of her nuns to the men's quarters, where she summoned a priest and asked him to go with her to the sufferer. On their arrival they saw that a crowd of people had gathered, who were trying without success to hold down the tormented man and restrain his convulsive movements. The priest pronounced exorcisms and did all he could to calm the poor man's frenzy, but even he, despite all his efforts, could achieve nothing. Just when it seemed that there was no remedy for his madness, the abbess suddenly thought of that sample of soil, and at once ordered a serving woman to go and fetch the casket in which it was kept. She brought it as ordered, and came into the porch of the house where the possessed man was writhing about in an inner room. He suddenly fell silent and as if lulled asleep laid down his head and relaxed all his limbs.

'All silent fell, and fixed their eager gaze' as they anxiously awaited the outcome. After about an hour, the man who was possessed sat up and said with a deep sigh: 'Now I feel well. I am restored to my senses.' They pressed him to tell them how it had happened, and he said: 'As soon as this maid came to the porch of the house, with the casket she was carrying, all the evil spirits that were troubling me disappeared and left me for ever.' The abbess then gave him a little of the soil, the priest said a prayer, and he spent a very peaceful night; and there was never again a night in which his old enemy returned to terrify or torment him.

✛

A LITTLE BOY IS CURED OF FEVER AT HIS TOMB

Some time after this there was in the same monastery a little boy who had been seriously ill for a long time with recurrent fevers. One day as he was anxiously expecting another attack, one of

Ecclesiastical History
Bk III, Ch 12

the brothers came in to him and said: 'Shall I tell you, my son, how you may be cured of this troublesome sickness? Get up and go into the church; go up to the tomb of Oswald, sit down there, and stay quiet next to the tomb. Make sure not to come out or move from your position until the time for the fever's return has passed. Then I will come in and bring you out.' He did as he had been advised, and while he sat by the saint's tomb the disease did not venture to touch him; on the contrary, so frightened was it that it disappeared and did not dare to afflict him on the second day or the third, or ever again. I was given this account by a brother from the monastery, who added that at the time when he spoke to me the boy on whom this miracle of healing had been performed was still living in the monastery, though now a young man. It is not surprising that the prayers of that king, who now reigns with the Lord, have great influence with Him, since during his reign as a king on earth he always gave the precedence, in his work and his prayers, to the Kingdom which is eternal.

It is said, for example, that he often remained at his prayers from the time of the office of matins until daybreak, and because of his frequent habit of prayer and giving thanks to God, wherever he sat he used to have his hands on his knees with the palms upwards. It is also widely believed, and has become proverbial, that he died with a prayer on his lips. When he saw that he was surrounded by the enemy forces and about to be slain, he prayed for the souls of his army; and this is the origin of the proverb, 'God have mercy on their souls, said Oswald falling to the ground.'

His bones, then, were transferred to the monastery and buried there, as we have said. The king who killed him ordered his head and hands with the arms to be severed from his body and fixed on stakes. The following year his successor Oswy arrived with an army and removed them, burying the head in the cemetery of the church of Lindisfarne but the hands and arms in the royal city.

'With the ebb and flow of the tide, this is a place that is twice a day encircled by the waves of the sea, like an island, and twice rejoined to the mainland when its shore becomes exposed again'

The traditional causeway — accessible by foot at low tide — across to Aidan's holy island of Lindisfarne.

✝

AFTER THE DEATH OF PAULINUS, ITHAMAR SUCCEEDS HIM
AS BISHOP OF HROFAESCAESTIR; ALSO THE WONDERFUL HUMILITY
OF KING OSWIN WHO IS CRUELLY MURDERED BY OSWY

*Ecclesiastical
History of the
English People*
Book III
Chapter 14

After Oswald had passed to the Kingdom of Heaven, he was succeeded in his earthly kingdom by his brother Oswy, a young man aged about thirty, who reigned for twenty-eight troubled years. He was attacked both by the heathen Mercians who had killed his brother and also by his own son Alchfrith and his nephew Aethelwald, the son of his brother and predecessor. In the second year of his reign, that is the year of our Lord 644, the most reverend father Paulinus, once bishop of Eboracum but later of Hrofaescaestir, departed to the Lord on the tenth of October, having held office as bishop for nineteen years, two months and twenty-one days. He was buried in the sanctuary of the church of the blessed apostle Andrew, which King Aethelbert built from its foundations in the city of Hrofaescaestir. To succeed him Archbishop Honorius consecrated Ithamar, a man of Kentish origin but in his life and his learning the equal of his predecessors.

At the start of his reign Oswy shared the kingly status with Oswin, of the family of King Edwin and a son of Osric, mentioned above. Oswin, a man of great piety and devotion, ruled the kingdom of Deira for seven years of great prosperity, and was loved by everyone. But even with him Oswy, who ruled the northern part of the land across the Humber, that is the kingdom of Bernicia, was unable to live at peace; and as the causes of their quarrel increased he murdered him in tragic circumstances. The two kings raised an army against each other, but Oswin saw that he could not go to war against an enemy who had stronger forces, and decided that it would be better for the present to abandon his intention of fighting and wait for more favourable times. He therefore dismissed the army he had raised at a place called Wilfaraesdun, meaning the hill of Wilfar, about ten miles to the north-west of the village of Cataracto; and he ordered them to return to their homes. He himself with only one loyal thane named Tondhere went to take refuge in the home of Hunwald, a nobleman whom he also believed to be a good friend. But sad to say, it proved far otherwise; for he and his thane were betrayed by the nobleman, and Oswy had them killed by his reeve Aethelwin, arousing universal disgust. The deed was done on the twentieth of August in the ninth year of his reign at a place called In Getlingum. Later on, to atone for his crime, a monastery was built there, in which prayers were to be offered daily to the Lord for the redemption of the souls of the two kings, both the one who was murdered and the one who ordered his murder.

King Oswin was tall and handsome, a man of pleasant conversation and courteous manners, and open-handed to people of high and low birth alike; as a result he was loved by everyone for the royal dignity which showed itself in his character, his bearing and his actions, and noblemen from almost every kingdom came together to serve in his retinue. He was graced and, one might say, especially blessed with the virtues that spring from self-denial and with none, it is said, more than humility, as a single example will show.

He had given an excellent horse to Bishop Aidan so that, although it was his custom to walk, he could ride it when he had to cross rivers or some other urgent necessity arose. Not long afterwards Aidan was met by a poor man begging for alms, and dismounted and ordered the horse, complete with its royal trappings, to be given to the beggar; for he was a man of great compassion and a friend of the poor, and like a father to those in need. When the king was told of this, he said to the bishop as they were going in to dinner: 'My Lord Bishop, why did you want to give the royal horse to a beggar? It would have been better for you to keep it as your own. Did we not have many less valuable horses, and other things which would have been good enough to give to the poor, without giving away the horse that I chose especially for your own use?' The bishop replied at once: 'What are you saying, Your Majesty? Surely that son of a mare is not more dear to you than that son of God?' With this, they went in to dinner. The bishop sat in his place, but the king, who had been hunting, stood by the fire with his thanes to get

'Aidan, a man of great gentleness, holiness and moderation'
The modern statue of Aidan beside the ruined Norman priory on Lindisfarne.

'The island of Hii ... is about five hides in area, according to English reckoning, and Columba's successors live there to this day'

Iona across the sound from Mull.

warm. As he warmed himself he remembered what the bishop had said to him, and suddenly unbuckled his sword and gave it to a thane, and then made haste to fall at the bishop's feet to ask his pardon. 'Never again,' he said, 'will I speak of this or pass judgement on what wealth of mine you should give to God's sons.' When the bishop saw this he was greatly alarmed, and stood up and lifted the king to his feet, assuring him that all was forgiven if only he would take his seat at dinner and banish his sorrow. The king, at the bishop's urgent bidding, recovered his good spirits, but the bishop for his part grew so sad that he burst into tears. He was asked by a priest in his native language, which the king and his retainers did not understand, why he wept, and said: 'I know that the king has not long to live. I have never before seen a humble king, and I therefore expect that he will soon be taken from this life; for this nation does not deserve to have such a ruler.' Not long after, the bishop's grim prophecy was fulfilled, as we have described, by the sad death of the king.

Bishop Aidan himself was taken from this world only eleven days after the murder of the king he loved, on the thirty-first of August, and received from the Lord the everlasting reward of his labours.

✠

BISHOP AIDAN FORETELLS A STORM TO SOME SAILORS, AND GIVES THEM HOLY OIL WITH WHICH TO CALM IT

Ecclesiastical History of the English People Book III Chapter 15

The God who judges our hearts revealed by miraculous signs how great was Aidan's worth, and it will be sufficient to put on record three of them. A priest named Utta, a most sincere and honest man and for that reason honoured by all, including the rulers of this world, was once sent to Kent to bring Eanfled, daughter of King Edwin, to marry King Oswy; she had been taken to Kent after her father's death. The priest intended to travel there by land but to return with the maiden by sea, and went to Bishop Aidan to beg him to pray to the Lord for his companions and himself at the start of their long journey. Aidan blessed them and commended them to the Lord, and also gave them some holy oil. 'I know,' he said, 'that when you have embarked on your ship a storm and adverse wind will rise up against you. But you, father, remember to pour this oil that I give you on to the sea, and then the winds will at once be stilled and you will enjoy a calm sea to return home by the way you wish.' All this happened just as the bishop had foretold. At first the waves of the sea were wild and the sailors tried to secure the ship by casting anchor, but all to no purpose. The waves swept over the ship from all sides and began to fill it, and everyone saw that death was at hand and expected to perish at any moment. Just then the priest, remembering the bishop's words, took the flask and poured the oil into the sea, and at once, as he foretold, its fury was stilled. So it came to pass that the man of God foretold the storm by the spirit of prophecy, and by the power of the same spirit made it calm again, though absent in body. I received the account of this miracle not from any unreliable source but from a most trustworthy priest of our church named Cynemund, who said that he had heard it from the priest Utta himself, on whom and through whom it was accomplished.

OVERLEAF

'They could not capture the town either by assault or by siege, and so attempted to destroy it by fire'

Bamburgh Castle at sunset.

✛

THE ENEMY ATTACK THE ROYAL TOWN WITH FIRE, BUT AIDAN SAVES IT BY PRAYER

Many people who were in a position to know tell of another miracle concerning St Aidan. During the time of his episcopate an enemy army of Mercians led by Penda laid waste the land of Northumbria far and wide with godless destruction, until they reached the royal town named after the former queen Bebba. They could not capture the town either by assault or by siege, and so attempted to destroy it by fire. They tore apart the small hamlets that they found in the neighbourhood and carried to the town a great mass of beams, rafters, partition walls, wattle and thatch, which they piled high round the wall on its landward side. When they saw the wind to be favourable, they started a fire in an attempt to burn down the town. At that time the most

Ecclesiastical History of the English People Book III Chapter 16

reverend Bishop Aidan was staying on Farne Island, about two miles from the town. He often used to go into retreat there to spend time in silent prayer, and in fact the site of his solitary dwelling is pointed out to this day. When he saw the tongues of fire and the smoke being carried by the wind over the town walls, he is said to have looked up to Heaven in tears and raised his hands, saying: 'See, Lord, the great evil that Penda does.' At these words the wind at once changed direction away from the town and hurled back the flames upon those who had kindled them. Some were injured and all were terrified, and they abandoned further assault on the town, realizing that it was under divine protection.

✟

THE BUTTRESS OF THE CHURCH ON WHICH HE WAS LEANING
WHEN HE DIED CANNOT BE DESTROYED BY THE FLAMES
WHEN THE REST OF THE BUILDING IS ON FIRE; HIS SPIRITUAL LIFE

Ecclesiastical History of the English People Book III Chapter 17

When the day arrived for him to depart this life after seventeen years as bishop, Aidan was on a royal estate not far from the town of which we have been speaking. He had a church and a cell there where he often used to stay, going out to preach in the surrounding countryside. This was his custom on other royal estates, where he had no property of his own except his church with its small plot of land. When he fell ill, therefore, they erected a tent for him at the west end of the church so that it was actually attached to the church wall; and so it came about that he breathed his last leaning on a buttress which supported the church on the outside. He died in the seventeenth year of his episcopate, on the thirty-first of August. His body was taken across shortly afterwards to the island of Lindisfarne and buried in the brothers' cemetery; but some time later, when a larger church had been built there, consecrated in honour of the most blessed chief of the apostles, his bones were transferred to it and buried on the right of the altar with the respect due to so great a bishop.

He was succeeded as bishop by Finan, who was also sent

from the Irish island monastery of Hii, and who held office for a considerable time. A few years later Penda, king of the Mercians, invaded the region, destroying everything he could by fire and sword, and the village in which Aidan died, including the church, was burnt down. But, miraculously, only the buttress on which he was leaning when he died could not be destroyed by the flames, though they devoured everything around it. When the miracle became known, the church was quickly rebuilt on the same spot and the same buttress used to support the wall on the outside as before. Some time afterwards it again happened that the village together with the church was destroyed by fire, this time through carelessness. But on that occasion also the flames were powerless to touch the buttress, and it was a great miracle indeed that, while they licked through the very nail-holes by which it was attached to the building, they were not permitted to damage it in any way. Consequently, when a third church was built there they set up that buttress not, as before, outside as a support for the building, but inside the church itself in memory of the miracle, so that those who came in might kneel and pray for Heaven's mercy. It is well known that from that time many people have obtained the grace of healing at that place; and many also by cutting off splinters from the buttress and putting them in water, have found it a means of curing the ailments of themselves and their families.

I have written this account of Aidan's character and life without in any way commending or approving his inaccurate knowledge of the observance of Easter. On the contrary, this is something that I abhor, as I have shown very clearly in my book on chronology; but as a truthful historian I have given a straight-forward account of his deeds and of events associated with him, giving praise where due to his way of life and setting it on record for the benefit of my readers. He cultivated peace and love, self-discipline and humility. His heart had the mastery over anger and avarice, and was contemptuous of pride and vain-glory. He spared no effort in carrying out and teaching the commands of Heaven, and was diligent in his reading and keeping of vigils. He showed the authority befitting a bishop in rebuking the proud and mighty, and was merciful in bringing comfort to the weak and relief and protection to the poor. In brief, as far as we have discovered from those who knew him, he neglected none of the duties that he learned from the writings of the evangelists, apostles and prophets, but strove with all his strength to fulfil them in his life. For these qualities the bishop wins my heartfelt admiration, since I know them to have been pleasing to God. However, as to his habit of observing Easter at the wrong time, whether in ignorance of the canonical time or because, though aware of it, he disregarded it out of deference to his race, this I neither approve nor commend. This much, even so, I can approve; that in the celebration of his own Easter he had at heart the same faith, and worshipped and preached the same mystery as we, namely the redemption of the human race through the passion, resurrection and ascension into Heaven of the one mediator between God and men, even the man Christ Jesus. This is why he did not, as some wrongly suppose, follow the Jews in keeping Easter on the fourteenth day of the moon whatever the day, but always kept it on the Lord's Day between the fourteenth and the twentieth day of the moon: he had faith in the Lord's resurrection, which he believed to have occurred on the day after the Sabbath, and hope of our resurrection, which he was convinced would also occur on the day after the Sabbath, now known as the Lord's Day. In these beliefs he was at one with holy Church.

'A dispute arises ...'

The Council of Whitby

Even as Bede writes of the martyrdom of Oswald and the dark days of Penda's onslaught on Northumbria, his chronicle foreshadows an event of much greater importance for the historian monk of Jarrow than much of the political and military turbulence that he recorded. That event was the Council of Whitby in the year 664.

Oswy, established as the new *Bretwalda* after his conquest of Penda's legions and elimination of Oswin of Deira, was the man who brought the great divide of the Church to its resolution at Whitby. Oswy's wife, Eanfled — King Edwin's daughter educated in the Kentish Church — celebrated Easter on the day appointed by papal edicts that had never reached the Celtic Church. Oswy, like his Iona-educated brother, followed the date for Easter set by the calendar of ancient Celtic tradition. The domestic difficulty of members of the same royal family celebrating the great Christian festival on different days is not hard to appreciate. Oswy's queen was — it seems — a lady of some persuasion, for she prevailed on her husband to grant the land for a monastery near Richmond at Gilling — Bede's In Getlingum — as penance for the murder of Oswin.

It was Abbess Hild's foundation at Whitby, known to Bede as Streanaeshalch, that was chosen by Oswy for the great debate to resolve the question of the date of Easter — and the related controversy prompted by Rome's insistence on the 'crown of thorns' form of monastic tonsure — in a council that brought the Celtic adherents from Lindisfarne face to face with those who followed the Roman orthodoxy.

It may seem to the modern reader that these were eccentric criteria over which to so bitterly divide the church. Perhaps the Victorian Bishop Lightfoot of Durham, an eloquent admirer of the old Celtic Church, puts his finger on the real issue. The tonsure — says the good bishop — was 'a triviality' and the date of Easter a question 'of convenience rather than principle.' What was at stake at Whitby was political power, specifically the imposition of Roman authority on the church of the *Bretwalda's* kingdom of Northumbria.

Bede records the great debate in some detail and offers vivid portraits of the personalities involved as the forceful Wilfrid carried the Roman argument to win the day over Colman of Lindisfarne. Thus — in the words of Bishop Lightfoot — 'the yoke of Roman dictation was firmly riveted on the neck of the ancient Irish church.'

Bede himself was a committed enthusiast of the Roman orthodoxy, yet he still betrays something of his own sympathy for the Celtic tradition. He was, after all, a monk of Northumbria who would have known well those of Aidan's Lindisfarne, and his regard for all things Irish disposed him well enough towards the Celtic spirit, even though his obedience to the Roman ways prompted his disapproval of Celtic practice.

Looking back over the centuries it is not easy for us to appreciate the full moment of the dispute at Whitby, but it is not difficult to respond to Bede's evocative portrait of the vanquished Colman, journeying from Lindisfarne into the northern mists on his long road back to the sacred isle of Iona.

✝

AFTER KING PENDA IS SLAIN, THE KINGDOM OF MERCIA RECEIVES THE FAITH OF CHRIST; AND OSWY, IN GRATITUDE FOR GAINING THE VICTORY, GIVES ESTATES AND LANDS TO GOD FOR BUILDING MONASTERIES

Ecclesiastical History of the English People Book III Chapter 24

At this time King Oswy was being harried beyond endurance by the savage attacks of Penda, king of the Mercians, whom I have often mentioned, and who had killed his brother. Finally Oswy was forced to promise that he would give him a vast quantity of royal treasures and gifts, precious beyond belief, as the price of peace, on condition that Penda would return home and cease from his utter devastation of the kingdoms under his rule. The faithless king, who had determined to destroy and exterminate his entire people from the humblest to the greatest, refused to agree to his proposal, and Oswy looked to the help of God's mercy to save him from the merciless heathen. He made a vow: 'If the heathen will not receive our gifts, let us offer them to Him who will, the Lord our God.' So he vowed that if the victory should be his, he would offer to the Lord his daughter to be dedicated to the life of holy virginity, and also that he would give twelve small estates to build monasteries; and with this, he went to battle with a very small army. It is said, in fact, that the heathen had an army thirty times as great; for they had thirty legions experienced in war and led by noble commanders, whom King Oswy and his son Alchfrith confronted with an insignificant force, as I have said, but trusting in Christ to lead them. Oswy's other son, Egfrith, was held hostage at that time by Queen Cynwise in the kingdom of the Mercians; while Aethelwald, son of King Oswald, who should have helped them, was on the enemy side, leading them against his native land and his own uncle. When battle was joined, however, Aethelwald withdrew from the fray and awaited the outcome in a place of safety. So the battle commenced, and the heathen were put to flight and cut down. The thirty royal commanders who had come to their aid were almost all killed, including Aethelhere, brother and successor of King Anna of the East Angles; and the cause of the war himself was slain with the loss of his thanes and followers. The battle was fought near the river Winwaed, which owing to heavy rain at the time had overflowed its banks and flooded a wide area of land around its course; so that the water claimed many more victims in the rout than the sword destroyed in battle.

In fulfilment of his vow to the Lord, and in gratitude to God for granting him the victory, King Oswy then gave his daughter Aelffled, who was barely a year old, to be dedicated to Him in perpetual virginity; and he further made a grant of twelve small estates where, withdrawn from the pursuit of earthly warfare, communities of monks might devote themselves to the religious life in the service of Heaven and pray that his people might enjoy everlasting peace. He granted six of these small estates in the kingdom of Deira and six in the kingdom of Bernicia; and each estate was of ten hides, so that there were one hundred and twenty hides in all. King Oswy's daughter Aelffled, now dedicated to God, entered the monastery named Heruteu, meaning the island of the hart, which was then governed by Abbess Hild. Two years later, Hild obtained an estate of ten hides at a place called Streanaeshalch, and built a monastery there; and the king's daughter became first a disciple there in the life of the Rule and later a teacher, until at the age of about sixty the blessed virgin entered into union with her heavenly bridegroom. She was buried in this monastery, as were her father Oswy, her mother Eanfled, her maternal grandfather Edwin, and many other nobles, in the church of St Peter the Apostle. King Oswy brought this war to an end in the district of Loidis in the thirteenth year of his reign on the fifteenth of November, to the great benefit of both peoples; for he freed his own people from devastation at the hands of the heathen enemy, and converted the Mercian people themselves and the people of the neighbouring kingdoms, having cut off the heathen head, to a state of grace in the Christian faith.

The first bishop to be appointed in the kingdom of Mercia, and also in Lindsey and the kingdom of the Middle Angles, was Diuma, as mentioned above, who died and was buried among the Middle Angles. The second was Ceollach, an Irishman like Diuma, who retired from the bishopric and returned to the Irish. The third was Trumhere, of English race but educated and consecrated by the Irish, who was abbot of the monastery of In Getlingum. This was the place, as mentioned above, where King Oswin was killed. Queen Eanfled, his relation, to atone for his unjust death, had asked King Oswy to make a grant of land there to Christ's servant Trumhere, as he too was a kinsman of the dead king, for the building of a monastery; and in the monastery continual prayers were to be said for the eternal salvation of both kings, namely the one who was murdered and the one who ordered his murder. King Oswy ruled over the Mercian people and the other peoples of the southern kingdoms for three years after King Penda was slain; and he also brought most of the Pictish people under English rule.

'It was arranged that a council should be held in the monastery called Streanaeshalch, meaning bay of the lighthouse.'

Sunset through the medieval abbey ruins at Whitby.

At this time he gave to Penda's son Peada the kingdom of the Southern Mercians, as he was his kinsman. This people occupy territory said to consist of five thousand hides and separated by the river Trent from the Northern Mercians, whose land extends to seven thousand hides. But the following spring Peada was treacherously murdered, betrayed, it is said, by his own wife at the very time of the Easter festival. Three years after King Peada's death, Mercian leaders named Immin, Eafa and Eadbert rebelled against King Oswy and set up as their king Penda's young son Wulfhere, whom they had kept in hiding. They drove out the rulers appointed by the foreign king, and bravely

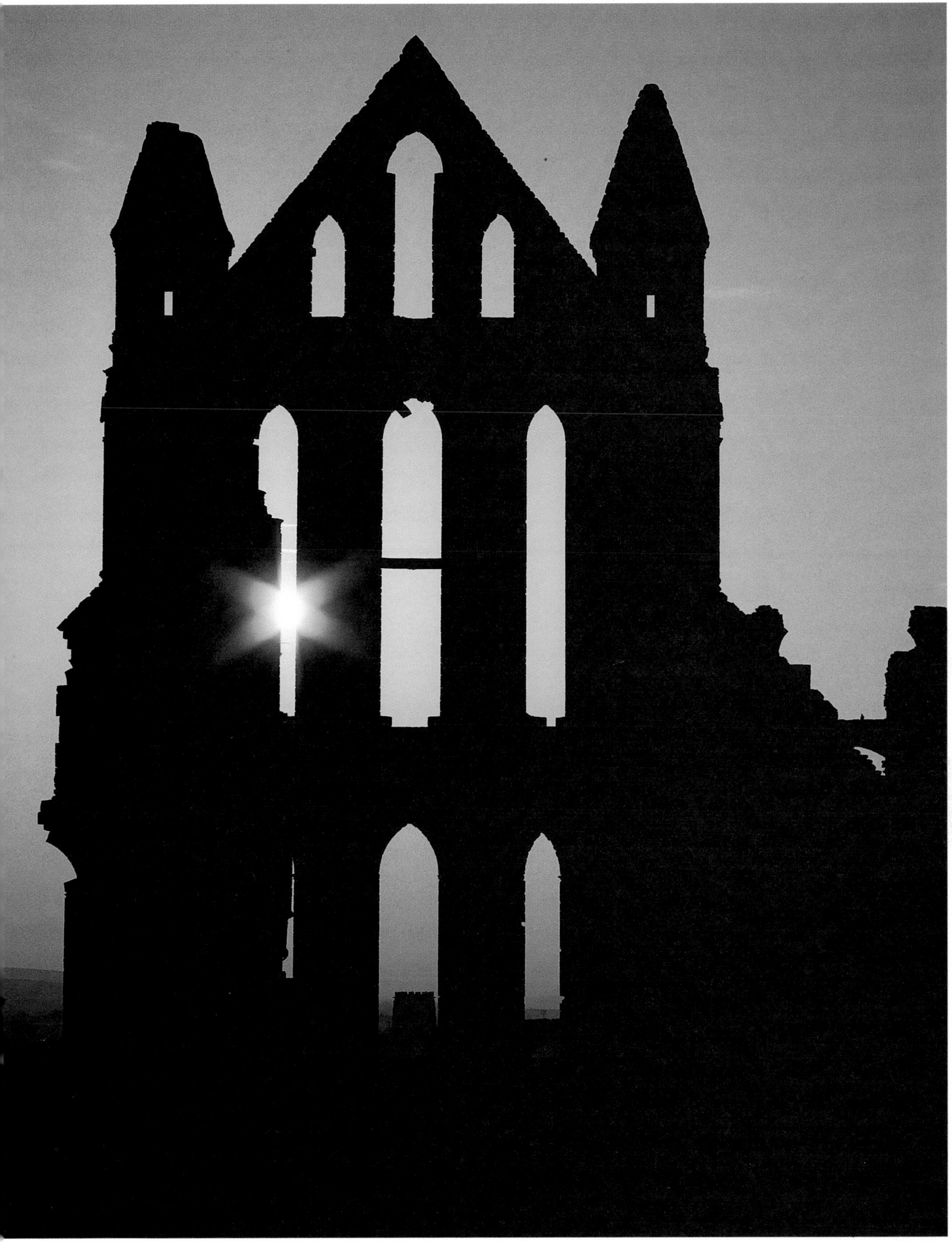

recovered both their lands and their freedom; and so, a free people with their own king, they rejoiced to serve Christ, their true king, for the sake of an everlasting kingdom in Heaven. King Wulfhere ruled over the Mercian people for seventeen years. His first bishop was Trumhere, mentioned above, his second Jaruman, his third, Chad, and his fourth, Winfrith. All these in succession were bishops of the Mercians under King Wulfhere.

✛

A DISPUTE ARISES WITH THOSE WHO CAME FROM IRELAND CONCERNING THE DATE OF EASTER

Ecclesiastical History of the English People Book III Chapter 25

Meanwhile, after Bishop Aidan had departed this life Finan had succeeded him as bishop, having been consecrated and sent by the Irish. On the island of Lindisfarne he built a church befitting an episcopal see, although he constructed it in the Irish manner entirely of hewn oak, not of stone, and thatched it with reeds; and it was later consecrated by the most reverend Archbishop Theodore to the honour of the blessed apostle Peter. However, Bishop Eadbert of Lindisfarne had the thatch removed and the whole church, that is to say not only the roof but the walls as well, covered with sheets of lead.

At this time there arose serious and recurrent controversy about the date of Easter. Those who had come from Kent and Gaul declared that the Irish observance of Easter Sunday was contrary to the practice of the universal Church. One particularly vigorous champion of the true Easter, named Ronan, was Irish by race but had been instructed in the authentic practice of the Church in Gaul or Italy. In his dispute with Finan he convinced many people, or at least spurred them to a more careful investigation of the truth, but he had no success at all in correcting Finan; on the contrary, being a man of headstrong temperament he made him embittered by his criticisms and turned him into an open opponent of the truth. James, once deacon of the venerable Archbishop Paulinus, observed the true, Catholic Easter along with all those that he could instruct in the better way.

Queen Eanfled, too, and her court, who had with her a priest from Kent named Romanus who followed the Catholic practice, observed Easter according to the tradition she had seen in Kent. As a consequence, it is said to have often come about in those days that Easter was celebrated twice in a single year, with the queen and her court still observing Lent and celebrating Palm Sunday at the very same time as the king had finished the fast and was keeping Easter Sunday. During the lifetime of Aidan, this disagreement about the keeping of Easter was borne with patience by everyone, because they knew full well that although he could not keep Easter otherwise than according to the practice of those who had sent him, nevertheless those works of faith, piety and love that he set himself diligently to perform were true to the practice of all the saints. He was therefore deservedly loved by everyone, even those who held different opinions about Easter; and not only ordinary people but bishops, too, like Honorius of Canterbury and Felix of East Anglia, held him in reverence.

After the death of his successor Finan, another Irishman, Colman, became bishop, and a serious controversy arose not only about the observance of Easter but about other matters of church discipline. This dispute naturally troubled the minds and hearts of many people, who were afraid that after taking the name of Christian they were running or had run in vain. It came to the ears of the rulers themselves, King Oswy and his son Alchfrith. Oswy, who had been taught and baptized by the Irish and was also well versed in their language, believed that nothing could be better than their teaching; whereas Alchfrith had been taught the Christian faith by Wilfrid, a man of great learning, and knew that his teaching was really to be preferred to all the traditions of the Irish. For Wilfrid had once been to Rome to study the doctrine of the Church, and had spent a long time at Lugdunum with Dalfinus, archbishop of Gaul, from whom he had received the Church's tonsure in the form of a crown. It was for this reason that Alchfrith had given him a monastery with forty hides of land at a place named In Hrypum. This was a site that he had given for a monastery a little earlier to the followers of Irish ways; but afterwards, when given a choice, they preferred

XV ALLELUIA TENEATUR QUADRAGENSIMU, QUIBUSTEMPORI CANTICAMATU BUSDICATUR A COPASCHA TINISPRIMATER USQUEPEN TIASEXTANONA TECOSTEN QU ECUMALLELU SINEINTERMISI IADICANTUR UESPERAIAMAN ONEDICATUR AL TEFANA RESPON LELUIA TAMIN SORIAUERONUM PSALMISQUAM QUAMDICANTUR INRESPONSORI CUMALLELUIA IS APESTICOSTEN NISIAPASCAUSÇ AUTEMUSQUE ADPENTICUSTEN INCAPUDQUADRA QUALITERDIUINA GENSIMAEOM OPERAPERDIEM NIBUSNOCTIB3 AGANTUR CUMSEXPOSTE UTAITPROFE RIORIBUSPSAL TA SEPTIER MISTANTUMAD INDIELAUDE NOCTURNASDICA DIXITIBI QUISEP TUR OMNIUERO TINARIUSSACRA DOMINICAEXTRA TU NUMERUS

'The Rule established by the Fathers'

This earliest surviving manuscript of the Rule of Benedict dates from less than forty years after the Council of Whitby. It was almost certainly commissioned by Wilfrid during his exile in Mercia in the early eighth century and its scribe may even have been a member of Wilfrid's household.

Bodleian Library, Oxford: MS Hatton 48, f.29r

'Colman took those who wished to follow him and ... went first to the island of Hii, from where he had been appointed to preach the Word to the English'

St Martin's Cross, Iona.

to leave the place rather than change their practices, and he gave it to a man worthy of it by his teaching as well as his way of life. At that time Agilbert, bishop of the West Saxons, whom we have mentioned above, a friend of King Alchfrith and Abbot Wilfrid, had arrived in Northumbria, and spent some time there. At the request of Alchfrith he ordained Wilfrid priest in his own monastery. With him he had a priest called Agatho.

In consequence of the dispute that had arisen in Northumbria about Easter, and the tonsure, and other Church matters, it was arranged that a council should be held to settle the dispute in the monastery called Streanaeshalch, meaning bay of the lighthouse, whose abbess was at that time Hild, a woman devoted to God. It was attended by both kings, father and son; Bishop Colman with his clergy from Ireland; and Bishop Agilbert with the priests Agatho and Wilfrid. James and Romanus were on their side — while Abbess Hild and her followers were on the side of the Irish, which included the venerable Bishop Cedd; he had been ordained by the Irish long before and acted at that council as a most scrupulous interpreter for both sides.

King Oswy opened the discussion by saying that those who served one God ought to have one rule of life and not differ in the celebration of the heavenly sacraments, since they all hoped for one kingdom in Heaven; they ought rather to inquire which was the truer tradition, and all follow it together. He then told his bishop Colman to speak first and explain the usage that he followed, and its origin. Colman then said: 'This method of keeping Easter which I observe, I received from my superiors, who sent me here as bishop; and all our fathers, men beloved of God, are known to have followed the same observance. In case any should judge it a matter for contempt and reproach, it is recorded that this very same observance was followed by the blessed evangelist John, a disciple specially dear to the Lord, and by all the churches over which he presided.'

After Colman had spoken along these lines, the king told Agilbert to declare his method of observance, together with its origin and the authority he had for following it. Agilbert replied: 'I request that my disciple, the priest Wilfrid, may speak instead of me, as we are both of the same mind as the other followers of the Church's tradition who are seated here, and he can give a better and clearer explanation of our view in the English language than I can through an interpreter.'

Then Wilfrid was bidden to speak by the king, and began thus: 'The Easter that we observe is the one we saw celebrated by everyone at Rome, where the blessed apostles Peter and Paul lived, taught, suffered and were buried. It is a usage we found to be universal in Italy and in Gaul, lands that we have travelled over for the purpose of study and prayer. In Africa, Asia, Egypt, Greece, and every part of the world, where the Church of Christ is scattered, we learned that this practice is followed by different nations speaking different languages, and all at one and the same time. The only exceptions are this people and their accomplices in stubbornness, I mean the Picts and the Britons, who from these two remotest islands in the Ocean, and from only parts of them, pursue a foolish struggle against the whole world.'

To these words of his Colman replied: 'I find it remarkable that you choose to call our struggle foolish, when we follow the example of that great apostle who was worthy to recline upon his Lord's breast, and who, as all the world knows, lived a life of great wisdom.'

Wilfrid answered: 'Far be it from us to reproach John with foolishness. He observed to the letter the decrees of the Law of Moses at a time when the Church still followed Jewish practice in many matters. The apostles were not able to abolish at a stroke the entire observance of the Law ordained by God, in the same way as there is an obligation on all who come to the faith to renounce idols invented by devils. They were afraid to create a stumbling-block for those Jews who were dispersed among the gentiles. It was for this reason that Paul circumcized Timothy, that he sacrificed victims in the temple, and that with Aquila and Priscilla he shaved his head at Corinth; the only purpose being to avoid scandalizing the Jews. It was for this reason that James said to Paul: "Thou seest, brother, how many thousands there are among the Jews of them which have believed; and they are all zealous for the Law."

'Yet today, now that the Gospel shines brightly through the

world, it is not necessary, or even lawful, for the faithful to be circumcized or to offer God sacrifices of flesh and blood. John, therefore, began the celebration of Easter according to the practice of the Law, in the evening of the fourteenth day of the first month, regardless of whether it fell on the Sabbath or any other day. But when Peter was preaching at Rome, remembering that the Lord rose from the dead, and brought to the world the hope of resurrection, on the day after the Sabbath, he realized that Easter should be kept according to the following rule: following the custom and precepts of the Law, he always waited for the rising of the moon in the evening of the fourteenth day of the first month, just as John did; if the Lord's Day, which was then called the first after the Sabbath, was to fall on the morning after the moon's rising, he began to celebrate Easter on that evening, as we all do today; but if the Lord's Day was not due on the morning after the fourteenth day of the moon, but on the sixteenth or seventeenth or any other day up to the twenty-first, he waited for it, and began the solemn rites of Easter the night before, on the evening of the Sabbath, so that Easter Sunday was always kept between the fifteenth and the twenty-first day of the moon.

'This evangelical and apostolical tradition does not abrogate, but rather is the fulfilment of, the Law, in which it is decreed that the Passover should be observed between the evening of the fourteenth day of the moon in the first month and the evening of the twenty-first day of the moon in the same month. All the successors of blessed John in Asia since his death, and the whole Church throughout the world, have come to follow this observance. That this is the true Easter, and the only one to be celebrated by the faithful, was reaffirmed, and not newly decided, by the Council of Nicaea, as the history of the Church teaches us.

'From this evidence it is clear, Colman, that you follow neither the example of John, as you suppose, nor that of Peter, whose tradition you knowingly contradict, and that your observance of Easter accords with neither the Law nor the Gospel. For John, who kept Easter according to the decrees of the Law of Moses, attached no importance to the first day after the Sabbath;

'Hild obtained an estate of ten hides at a place called Streanaeshalch and built a monastery there'

The ruins of the medieval abbey at Whitby. The seventh-century foundations of Hild's monastery lie under the grass sloping away to the right of this photograph.

you differ from him in that you always celebrate Easter on the first day after the Sabbath. Peter celebrated Easter Sunday between the fifteenth and the twenty-first day of the moon; you, on the other hand, keep Easter Sunday between the fourteenth and the twentieth day of the moon, and often begin Easter in the evening of the thirteenth day. The Law makes no mention of this, and it was not on this day but on the fourteenth that the Lord who is the author and giver of the Gospel ate the old Passover in the evening, and instituted the sacraments of the New Testament for the Church to celebrate in commemoration of His passion. Again, the twenty-first day of the moon, which the Law particularly ordered to be observed, is completely excluded by your observance of Easter. So, as I have said, in your celebration of the greatest of festivals you agree neither with John, nor with Peter, nor with the Law, nor with the Gospel.'

Colman's reply was as follows: 'Did Anatolius, a holy man who was highly praised in that history of the Church that you refer to, and who wrote that Easter should be celebrated between the fourteenth and twentieth days of the moon, hold a belief contrary to the Law and the Gospel? Are we to believe that our most reverend father Columba and his successors, men beloved of God, who kept Easter in the same way, believed and acted contrary to the holy scriptures? There were many among them to whose holiness signs from Heaven and the miracles which they performed bore testimony. I have no doubt that they were saints, and I never cease to follow their way of life, their customs and their teaching.'

Wilfrid answered: 'We all agree that Anatolius was a most holy and learned man and worthy of the highest praise; but what have you to do with him, seeing that you fail even to follow his instructions? In his observance of Easter he followed a correct rule and established a cycle of nineteen years, which you are either unaware of or treat with contempt, though it is recognized and observed by the whole Church of Christ. He assigned the fourteenth day of the moon to Easter Sunday because he reckoned in the Egyptian manner and counted the evening of the fourteenth as the start of the fifteenth day. In the same way in assigning the twentieth day to Easter Sunday he included its latter part in the twenty-first. That you are ignorant of this distinction is proved by the fact that you sometimes quite clearly keep Easter before the full moon, that is on the thirteenth day of the moon.

'As regards your father Columba and his followers, whose holiness you claim to imitate and whose rule and teaching confirmed by signs from Heaven you claim to follow, I might reply that on the Day of Judgement there will be many saying to the Lord that they prophesied in His name, and cast out devils, and performed many miracles: but the Lord will reply that He never knew them. But far be it from me to say this about your fathers: it is much better to believe good than evil of those of whom nothing is known. So I will not deny that they were God's servants and beloved of God, who loved God in simple ignorance and pious intent. Nor do I think that their observance of Easter did them much harm, as long as no one had come to show them a more accurate tradition to follow; indeed, I believe that if any observer of the Catholic rule had come to them they would have followed his guidance, just as we know they followed all those of God's laws that came to their knowledge. You, however, and your supporters have heard the decrees of the Apostolic See, or rather of the universal Church, which are confirmed by the holy scriptures; and if you disdain to follow them there can be no doubt of your guilt. Your fathers may have been holy men, yet are they, a few men in one corner of a remote island, to have precedence over the universal Church of Christ throughout the world? Your father Columba, and ours, too, if he belonged to Christ, may have had miraculous powers, yet could he have precedence over the most blessed chief of the apostles, to whom the Lord said: "Thou art Peter, and upon this rock I will build my Church, and the gates of Hell shall not prevail against it, and I will give unto thee the keys of the Kingdom of Heaven"?'

After these closing words from Wilfrid, the king said: 'Is it true, Colman, that these words were spoken to Peter by the Lord?' Colman said: 'It is true, Your Majesty.'

The king asked: 'Can you produce any evidence that similar

authority was given to your father Columba?' He answered: 'None.' The king went on: 'Do you both agree without any question that these words were addressed chiefly to Peter, and that it was to him that the keys of the Kingdom of Heaven were given by the Lord?' They both answered: 'Yes.'

The king concluded as follows: 'Then I tell you that he is that keeper of the gate, and I will not contradict him. To the best of my knowledge and powers I desire to obey his commands in everything, in case when I come to the gates of the Kingdom of Heaven he, who by your testimony holds the keys, should turn away, and there be no one to open for me.'

When the king had spoken, all those who sat or stood there, both high and low, expressed their agreement; and they gave up their inaccurate observance and were quick to adopt what they now knew to be the better rule.

✢

AFTER HIS DEFEAT COLMAN RETURNS HOME, AND TUDA BECOMES BISHOP IN HIS PLACE; THE STATE OF THE CHURCH UNDER THESE TEACHERS

When the dispute had been ended and the assembly dissolved, Agilbert returned home. Seeing his teaching rejected and his principles discounted, Colman took those who wished to follow him and refused to accept the Catholic Easter and the tonsure in the form of a crown, about which there had also been much discussion, and went back to the Irish to discuss with his people what action to take about it. Cedd returned to his bishopric and abandoned Irish practices, accepting the Catholic observation of Easter. This debate occurred in the year of our Lord 664, which was the twenty-second year of Oswy's reign, and the thirtieth year of the Irish episcopate in England, as Aidan was bishop for seventeen years, Finan for ten, and Colman for three.

When Colman returned home he was succeeded as bishop of Northumbria by Christ's servant Tuda, who had been educated and consecrated bishop among the southern Irish and who, in accordance with the custom of that kingdom, had the ecclesiastical tonsure in the form of a crown and observed the Catholic

Ecclesiastical History of the English People Book III Chapter 26

'Elge, in the kingdom of the East Angles, ... derives its name from the large number of eels caught in the marshes.' Ely Cathedral.

rule for the time of Easter. He was a good and devout man but governed the Church for only a very short time. He had come from Ireland during Colman's episcopate, and was diligent in teaching all men, by his word and his example, the doctrines of the true faith. The brothers who preferred to stay in the church of Lindisfarne when the Irish departed were put under the charge of a new abbot, Eata, a most reverend and kindly man who was abbot of the monastery of Mailros. This is said to have been done by King Oswy at the special request of Colman before his departure, as Eata was one of twelve boys of English race whom Aidan took at the start of his episcopate to give a Christian education; and the king had great love for Bishop Colman because of his innate good sense. Eata was the same man who a little later became bishop of the church of Lindisfarne. Colman on his departure for home took with him some of the bones of the most reverend father Aidan, leaving the remainder in the church of which he had charge with the instruction that they be buried in its sanctuary.

Evidence of the great frugality and austerity practised by Colman and his predecessors was afforded by the place over which they ruled, for on their departure only a very few buildings were found there, apart from the church, consisting only of those necessary to any civilized community. They owned no wealth apart from their livestock, since any money they received from the rich was at once given to the poor. They had no need to save money or provide accommodation in order to receive the rulers of the world, who only came to the church for the purpose of prayer and to hear the word of God. The king himself, whenever the opportunity allowed it, came with only five or six thanes, and went away after completing his prayers in the church. Even if it chanced that they had a meal there they were content with the simple daily fare of the brothers, and asked for nothing more. The sole concern of the teachers of those days was to serve God, not the world, and to feed the soul, not the belly. The religious habit, therefore, was held in great respect at that time, so that whenever a cleric or monk appeared he was welcomed gladly by everyone as a servant of God. Even if one was discovered passing on the road, they would run up to him and bow their heads, and were glad to be signed with the cross by his hand or blessed by his lips; and they paid close heed to such men's exhortations. On the Lord's Day they gathered eagerly in the church or the monasteries, not to get food for their bodies but to listen to the word of God; and if a priest came by chance to their village the people at once came together, eager to receive from him the word of life. The priests and clerics themselves visited their villages for no other reason than to preach, baptize, visit the sick and, in sum, to care for their souls; and so free were they from any taint of avarice that none accepted grants of land and estates for building monasteries unless compelled by the secular rulers. For some time afterwards this continued to be the practice of all the churches in Northumbria. But enough has now been said on these matters.

AFTER LEAVING BRITAIN, BISHOP COLMAN FOUNDS TWO MONASTERIES IN IRELAND

Meanwhile Colman, who was a bishop from Ireland, left Britain and took with him all the Irish whom he had gathered on the island of Lindisfarne; and also about thirty men of English race, both groups being thoroughly instructed in the monastic way of life. Leaving some brothers in his church, he went first to the island of Hii, from where he had been appointed to preach the word to the English. He then withdrew to a small and remote island off the west coast of Ireland, called Inisboufind, meaning the island of the white heifer. On his arrival there he built a monastery and housed in it the monks whom he had assembled from both races and brought with him. They were unable to live in harmony with each other, as in summertime, when the harvest had to be gathered, the Irish left the monastery and strayed in different directions over the country which was familiar to them; yet they returned on the approach of winter, expecting to share in the supplies provided by the English. Colman, therefore, looked for a means of healing the dispute, and after searching everywhere far and near he found a place suitable for building a

Ecclesiastical History of the English People Book IV Chapter 4

monastery on the Irish mainland, called in the Irish language
Mag éo. He bought a small part of it to build a monastery on
from the nobleman to whose estate it belonged, on condition
that the monks who settled there should offer prayers to the
Lord for the provider of the land. The monastery was built at
once with the help of the nobleman and all his neighbours, and
Colman housed the English there, leaving the Irish on the island.
This monastery is still occupied by Englishmen. From its modest
beginning it has grown today into a large monastery, usually
called Muig éo, and its entire community were converted long
ago to better practices. It has an excellent company of monks,
gathered there from England, who live after the example of the
venerable fathers under a Rule and a canonically elected abbot,
in strict and devout self-denial and by the labour of their own
hands.

Etheldreda of Ely

With the chapters on the virgin saint of the fen country Bede's *Historia* first reaches his own time. St Etheldreda — or Aethelthryth in the Saxon form — established her nunnery at Ely in 673, the year of Bede's own birth.

Etheldreda was known to later centuries as St Audrey and in medieval times the fair that celebrated her name was notorious for its sale of cheap finery known as 'St Audrey's Lace.' Corrupted to 'Tawdry Lace' it has bequeathed the less-than-complimentary adjective 'tawdry' to the modern dictionary, a sad memorial for a royal lady who must have been endowed with extraordinary character.

Bede tells how the devout Etheldreda maintained her virgin state through no less than two marriages. Her first spouse, a princeling of the fenland tribe known as the South Gyrwas, left her a widow and she was subsequently given in marriage to Egfrith, the son of Oswy. King Egfrith — perhaps not unreasonably — was distressed at the resolute failure of his lady to consummate their union, but eventually consented to his saintly queen's most heartfelt desire and granted her the freedom to become a nun. Etheldreda went first to the nunnery at Coldingham — Bede's Coludesbyrig — and went on to establish her own nunnery at Ely, known then as Elge.

It is interesting that the date of her foundation at Ely coincides with those of Wilfrid's at Hexham and Benedict Biscop's at Wearmouth and that the land for all three was granted by Egfrith. It seems more than likely that the king's generosity was prompted by his queen and that the Church owed no less than three major foundations to Etheldreda's powers of persuasion.

Etheldreda's virgin state was — Bede suggests — a source of wide-spread incredulity and he pursued the historical fact of the matter with Bishop Wilfrid whom Etheldreda had held in the highest regard. Wilfrid confirmed the story and told Bede how Egfrith had offered him 'land and great wealth' if he could persuade the queen of her marital duties.

Bede's researches into Etheldreda's history were probably also assisted by the brothers at Lastingham, with whom Etheldreda's steward Oswin settled when he left Egfrith's court to take the tonsure at the same time as his queen took the veil.

Etheldreda's standing as a saint was duly confirmed when her body was disinterred some sixteen years after her death in 679. The body was found to be not only incorrupt, but a scar from surgical treatment of a fatal tumour on her neck had healed over in death — to the amazement of the doctor who had attended her last hours.

Bede concludes his chronicle of Etheldreda with some verse of his own — an impressive hymn to virginity. Bede was skilled in the poet's art, both in Latin and in the Saxon vernacular, and his elegant eulogy to Etheldreda bears testimony to that accomplishment. It takes the acrostic form, in which the initial letters of the couplets form an alphabetical sequence through to the A-M-E-N initials of the last lines. A further poetic discipline closes each couplet with the same phrase with which it begins. Bede's hymn provides a fine and welcome poetic coda to his somewhat macabre history of the life, death and post-mortality of Etheldreda of Ely.

✣

QUEEN AETHELTHRYTH PRESERVES HER VIRGINITY, AND HER BODY CAN SUFFER NO CORRUPTION IN THE TOMB

Ecclesiastical History of the English People Book IV Chapter 19

King Egfrith married a wife named Aethelthryth, daughter of Anna the king of the East Angles; he was devoutly religious, and in all matters a man of exemplary character and life. She had been married before to an alderman of the Southern Gyrwas called Tondbert, but he had died shortly after and she was given in marriage to King Egfrith. Although she lived with him for twelve years, she preserved intact the glory of perpetual virginity. I enquired about this myself, when some had cast doubt on it, and was assured of its truth by Bishop Wilfrid of blessed memory, who said he had indisputable evidence of her virginity in that Egfrith had promised to give him lands and great wealth if he could persuade the Queen to consummate the marriage; for Egfrith knew that she loved no man more than Wilfrid. We must not doubt, when reliable historians tell that it happened from time to time in the past, that such a thing could happen in our time also, through the gift of that one Lord who promises to remain with us to the end of the world. Moreover, that miraculous sign from God whereby her flesh could not suffer corruption after her burial, is proof that she remained uncorrupted by contact with a man.

For a long time she had been asking the king for permission to leave behind the cares of the world and to serve Christ, the only true king, in a monastery; and when at last she obtained her request she entered the monastery of Abbess Ebba, an aunt of King Egfrith, at a place called Coludesbyrig, receiving the veil and habit of a nun from Bishop Wilfrid. A year later, she herself became an abbess in the district called Elge, where she built a monastery and became the virgin mother of many virgins dedicated to God, prefiguring the life of Heaven in her conduct and her teachings. They say of her that from the time when she entered the monastery she would never wear linen, but only woollen clothes; she would seldom take a hot bath, except on the eve of the greater festivals such as Easter, Pentecost and Epiphany, and even then last of all, after Christ's other handmaidens who were present had washed first, assisted by her and her attendants. She seldom ate more than one meal a day, except on the greater festivals or when in exceptional need; she always, unless prevented by serious illness, stayed in church intent on her prayers from the time of the office of matins until daybreak. There are also those who say that through the spirit of prophecy she foretold the plague by which she was to die, and revealed to the whole community the number of those from her monastery who were to be taken by the plague from the world. She was taken to the Lord in the presence of her community seven years after becoming abbess, and by her own command was buried in a wooden coffin, taking her place among the others in accordance with the time of her death.

Her successor in the office of abbess was her sister Seaxburg, who had been the wife of Earconbert, king of Kent. Sixteen years after Aethelthryth's burial, the new abbess decided that her bones should be raised and placed in a new coffin and transferred to the church. She ordered some of the brothers to search for stone from which to make a coffin for this purpose, and they set off in a boat, as the district of Elge is completely surrounded by water and marshes and has no large stones. They came to a small deserted city not far away, called in English Grantacaestir, and near its walls they soon found a coffin beautifully made out of white marble, together with a close-fitting lid of the same stone. Realizing from this that the Lord had prospered their journey, they gave thanks to Him and took the coffin back to the monastery.

When the tomb of the holy virgin and bride of Christ was opened and her body brought out into the light, it was found to be as free from corruption as if she had died and been buried that very day. This is testified by Bishop Wilfrid and many others who knew about it, but even surer proof is provided by Cynefrith the doctor, who was present both at her death and at her raising from the tomb. He used to relate how during her illness she had a very large tumour under her jaw.

'They told me,' he said, 'to make an incision in the tumour to drain off the poisonous matter inside it; and when I did so, for two days she seemed a little easier, so that many thought she might recover from her sickness. On the third day, however, she suffered a recurrence of the pain and was soon taken from the world, leaving behind all pain and death in exchange for the health of everlasting life.

'When, after all those years, her bones were about to be raised from the tomb, they spread a tent above it and the whole congregation stood round it chanting, the brothers on one side and the sisters on the other, while the abbess herself went inside with a few helpers to bring out and wash the bones. Suddenly we heard the abbess cry out inside in a loud voice: "Glory to the name of the Lord." Shortly after, they drew back the entrance to the tent and called me in, and I saw, raised from the tomb and placed on a bed, the body of God's holy virgin seeming to be asleep. They also removed the covering from her face, and showed me that even the wound caused by the incision I had made was healed, so that, strange to tell, instead of the open, gaping wound with which she had been buried there now appeared only the faintest traces of a scar. All the linen cloths, too, in which her body had been wrapped, looked as fresh and new as if they had been put round her chaste limbs that very day.'

It is also said that when she was afflicted by this tumour and the pain in her jaw and neck, she welcomed suffering of this kind and used to say: 'I know for sure that I deserve the weight of suffering that I bear in my neck, for I remember how as a young girl I used to load it with the frivolous weight of jewellery. I believe that God in His mercy has willed that I should endure the pain in my neck that I might be absolved from the guilt of idle vanity. So instead of gold and pearls, my neck now boasts a burning red tumour.' The touch of those linen cloths was effective in driving out devils from the bodies of those they possessed, and from time to time in curing other illnesses. They say that the coffin, too, in which she was first buried, healed many sufferers from diseases of the eyes; they put their heads against the coffin and said a prayer, and at once were rid of the pain or failing sight which troubled them. So the maidens washed her body, wrapped it in new robes, carried it into the church, and laid it in the sarcophagus which had been brought; and it lies there to this day and is held in great reverence. Marvellous to relate, the sarcophagus was found to fit the virgin's body as perfectly as if it had been specially made for her; and the space for the head, which was fashioned separately, appeared to have been shaped exactly to the size of her head.

Elge, in the kingdom of the East Angles, has an area of about six hundred hides, and resembles an island, being surrounded, as we have said, by marshes and water; and it derives its name from the large number of eels caught in the marshes. Christ's handmaiden wished to have her monastery there because, as we have said, her own ancestors came from the kingdom of the East Angles.

A HYMN ABOUT HER

It seems fitting to include in this history a hymn to virginity, which I composed in the elegiac metre many years ago. It gives praise and honour to this same queen and bride of Christ, truly therefore a queen because the bride of Christ; and I follow the practice of holy scripture, in whose narrative, as is well known, many songs are inserted composed in metrical verses.

Ecclesiastical History of the English People Book IV Chapter 20

All-gracious Three in One, ruler of all the ages,
    Assist my song, All-gracious Three in One.
Battles be Virgil's theme, the gifts of peace be mine;
    Christ's bounty mine, battles be Virgil's theme.
Chaste be the song I sing, not faithless Helen's rape:
    Lust for the lustful, chaste be the song I sing.
Divine the gifts I tell, not piteous Troy's travail;
    For Earth's delight divine the gifts I tell.
Eternal God comes down to holy virgin's womb,
    To free mankind, eternal God comes down.
From virgin mother pure the world's creator's born,
    Mary, God's gate, from virgin mother pure.
Glad sings the virgin choir the Lord of Thunder's birth
    From virgin's womb: glad sings the virgin choir.
Her glory sowed the seed of virgins yet unborn,
    Of virgin flowers her glory sowed the seed.
In fiercest flames consumed stood virgin Agatha,
    Eulalia stood, in fiercest flames consumed.
King of the beasts unthrones chaste Tecla's high resolve,
    Euphemia chaste king of the beasts unthrones.
Laughing they face the sword, stronger than steel their faith,
    Agnes and Cecily, laughing they face the sword.
Many's the triumph won by purity of heart,
    Through all the world many's the triumph won.
Now our days too hath blest a noble virgin's life,
    Bright Aethelthryth now our days too hath blest.
Of mighty father born, and glorious royal line,
    Nobler with God, of mighty father born.
Proud on her royal throne she reigned on earth, and lives
    Beyond the stars proud on her royal throne.
Queen, should'st thou seek a man, vowed to thy Lord on
       high,
    To Christ betrothed, Queen, should'st thou seek a man?
Ruler of Heaven's mother now thy guide, thou too
    May be thyself Ruler of Heaven's mother.
Spouse to the Lord betrothed, for twelve years had she
       reigned,
    In holy walls spouse to the Lord betrothed.

To Heaven dedicate a heavenly life she spent;
    Her soul returned, to Heaven dedicate.

Under the earth her flesh sixteen Novembers lay,
    All incorrupt under the earth her flesh.

Xrist Jesus, by thy power her very shroud in earth
    Inviolate shines, Xrist Jesus by thy power.

Yea, the black serpent yields before that sacred shroud,
    Pestilence flies, yea, the black serpent yields.

Zealously chafes the foe, who once had conquered Eve;
    By virgin vanquished, zealously chafes the foe.

About thee, bride of God, on earth what glory shines;
    Heaven's light shall shine about thee, bride of God.

Many thy blessed gifts, bright gleams the wedding torch;
    See, the Groom comes: many thy blessed gifts.

Ever new songs are thine to sweet harp's melody,
    To hymn thy Lord ever new songs are thine.

None keeps thee from the Lamb in highest Heaven
      enthroned,
    Virgin most pure, none keeps thee from the Lamb.

'A hymn to virginity which I composed in the elegiac metre many years ago ... gives praise and honour to this same queen'

Bede's hymn to Etheldreda from the Moore manuscript of the *Historia*. The acrostic alphabet and amen are clearly discernible.

Cambridge University Library: MS Kk 5 16ff 86v/87r

Abbess Hild and Caedmon

Without Bede's *Historia* we would know virtually nothing of the Abbess Hild — Hilda of Whitby — who ranks with Etheldreda among the women pre-eminent in the Church of seventh-century Northumbria.

Hild, like Etheldreda, was high-born. Bede tells us that she was the daughter of a nephew of Edwin of Deira and baptized by Paulinus at the same time as Edwin. She followed a secular life until the age of thirty-three when she travelled to Gaul to take the habit in the nunnery at Cale — Chelles, near Paris — from where she was summoned back by Bishop Aidan.

On her return, she settled first at a nunnery on Wearside before moving on to Heruteu — known today as Hartlepool — where she followed Heiu as abbess of what was apparently a dual foundation of nunnery and monastery under the same rule. From Hartlepool she went on to Whitby — Bede's Streanaeshalch — where Oswy had granted land for a similar dual foundation in gratitude for his victory over Penda on the banks of the Winwaed in the year 655. It was at Streanaeshalch that Aelffled, Oswy's daughter who had been dedicated to the Church at just one year old as a further offering of gratitude for the victory on the Winwaed, eventually succeeded Hild as abbess. We know that Aelffled ruled the foundation, jointly with her mother Eanfled after the death of Oswy, in the years after Hild. Whitby may well have thrived for another hundred years, at least until the onset of the Viking raids, but we know little more of it after Bede until its revival under the Normans.

There is some irony attached to Oswy's choice of Hild's Streanaeshalch as the site of the great debate of 664, because that foundation had always honoured the ways of Iona rather than Rome. The 'Rule' by which Hild governed her community at Whitby was certainly that of Columba rather than Benedict. Hild herself had been a protégé of Aidan, educated in the Irish tradition, and Bede has already confirmed for us that her own sympathies lay with Colman's side. Yet it is the Whitby of Abbess Hild that history has remembered as the place where the Celtic Church in Northumbria was at last laid low.

The ruins of the medieval monastery are still to be seen high on the cliff at Whitby and archaeological excavations suggest that the Saxon monastic buildings occupied much the same site. Streanaeshalch never achieved the reputation for art and learning that so distinguished Lindisfarne, Wearmouth and Jarrow, but it must have held a position of some importance in the Deiran province of Northumbria.

That importance doubtless lay in its educational role. No less than five future bishops were trained there, notably Wilfrid of Hexham and John of Beverley, but Whitby's greatest son was a common herdsman known still as the first English poet. His name was Caedmon and Bede tells us how he was inspired by a miraculous vision to hymn the Creator in the Saxon tongue.

Bede — always keen to record a miracle — offers an account of Caedmon which affirms Whitby's educational importance. It is not difficult to imagine the evangelical impact of sacred verse — inspired by a miracle, written in the language of the ordinary people and reflecting the ancient tradition of Saxon oral poetry — on the illiterate, probably semi-pagan, population of seventh-century Northumbria. It is interesting to note that the earliest manuscripts of Bede's chapter on Caedmon transcribe his hymn in the original Anglo-Saxon alongside Bede's Latin rendering of the verse.

✛

THE LIFE AND DEATH OF ABBESS HILD

In the following year, the year of our Lord 680, Christ's most devout servant Hild, the abbess of the monastery called Streanaeshalch, as previously mentioned, was taken from this earth on the seventeenth day of November, to enjoy the reward of heavenly life after all the works of Heaven that she performed on earth. She lived for sixty-six years, and her life fell into two equal parts: for the first thirty-three years she spent a noble life in the secular habit, while the second half she dedicated yet more nobly to the Lord in the monastic life. For she was of noble birth, daughter of King Edwin's nephew Hereric, and in company with Edwin she received the faith and mysteries of Christ during the mission of Paulinus of blessed memory, the first bishop of the Northumbrians; and she preserved that faith inviolate until judged worthy to see Him face to face.

After resolving to retire from secular life and serve Him alone, she withdrew to the kingdom of the East Angles to whose king she was related. She wished if possible to leave her home

Ecclesiastical History of the English People
Book IV
Chapter 23

and all her possessions and cross over to Gaul, where she intended to live as an exile for the Lord's sake in the monastery of Cale, the more easily to earn an everlasting home in Heaven. In the same monastery at that time her sister Hereswith, mother of Aldwulf the king of the East Angles, was living by the monastic Rule and awaiting her eternal crown; and inspired by her example Hild remained in that kingdom a whole year intending to travel abroad. However, she was then summoned home by Bishop Aidan and given land one hide in area to the north of the river Wear, where she lived the monastic life for a further year with a small number of companions.

After this she became abbess of the monastery of Heruteu, founded a little earlier by Christ's devout servant Heiu, who is said to have been the first woman in the kingdom of the Northumbrians to take the vows and habit of the religious life, when she was ordained by Bishop Aidan. Not long after the monastery's foundation Heiu left for the city of Calcaria, which the English call Kaelcacaestir, and made her home there; and Christ's servant Hild was appointed to take charge of the monastery. She at once set about ordering all its life according to a Rule, following the guidance of learned men; for Bishop Aidan and other devout men who knew her, in recognition of her innate wisdom and devotion to God's service, used to visit her frequently in heartfelt affection and give her careful instruction.

After having charge of this monastery for some years, preoccupied with maintaining the life of the Rule, she was appointed also to found or set in order a monastery at a place called Streanaeshalch, and carried out her task with energy. She established the discipline of the same monastic Rule as in her previous monastery, and there too she taught the strict observance of justice, holiness and chastity and all the virtues, but especially peace and charity; and in imitation of the early Church there was no one rich or in need there, for they held all things in common and nothing was regarded as anyone's private possession. Such was her own good sense that her advice was sought and obtained not only by ordinary folk in difficulties but often too by kings and rulers. She required those under her to devote so much time to reading the holy scriptures and to the practice of good works that there were many in that community found fit to enter holy orders and the service of the altar.

For example, we have seen five members of that monastery go on to become bishops, all of them men of exceptional worth and holiness; their names are Bosa, Aetla, Oftfor, John and Wilfrid. Of the first of these we have mentioned earlier that he was consecrated bishop of Eboracum; of the second we must briefly remark that he was consecrated bishop of Dorciccaestra; and of the last two, consecrated respectively bishop of Hagustaldesea and bishop of Eboracum, we must speak below. Of Oftfor we may say at this point that he devoted himself to the reading and observance of the scriptures in both of Abbess Hild's monasteries, but at length in search of still greater perfection went to Kent to Archbishop Theodore of blessed memory. After spending some time there in the study of sacred texts he also undertook the journey to Rome, which at that time was regarded as especially meritorious. Returning from Rome to Britain, he visited the kingdom of the Hwiccas, then ruled by King Osric, and stayed there a long time preaching the word of the faith and setting an example of holy living to those who saw and heard him. At the time the bishop of that kingdom, whose name was Bosel, was so burdened by ill health that he could not fulfil his episcopal duties himself, and so by general consent Oftfor was chosen bishop in his place and at the bidding of King Aethelred consecrated by Bishop Wilfrid of blessed memory. Wilfrid at that time was acting as bishop of the Middle Angles, as Archbishop Theodore had died and no one had yet been appointed bishop to succeed him. Shortly before God's servant Bosel became bishop, Tatfrith, a man of great energy and learning and of outstanding ability, was chosen to be bishop of that kingdom, and he also was from Abbess Hild's monastery; but before he could be consecrated his life was cut short by an untimely death.

Abbess Hild, then, the handmaid of Christ, who was called mother by all who knew her for her exceptional devotion and grace, not only set a pattern of life for the community in her own monastery but also enabled many who lived further afield, and who had heard the happy report of her industry and virtue, to obtain salvation and repentance. This was in fulfilment of a dream which her mother Breguswith had when Hild was in her infancy. While her husband Hereric was in exile under the king of the Britons, Cerdic, where he later died by poison, she had a dream in which he was suddenly taken from her, and though she searched for him with the utmost care no trace of him could be found anywhere. However, after searching thoroughly she suddenly found under her dress a most precious necklace; and as she examined it more closely it seemed to shine with such a blaze of light that it filled all the land of Britain with the beauty of its radiance. There is no doubt that this dream was fulfilled in her daughter, of whom we are speaking, since her life afforded examples of the works of light not only for herself but for many others who wished to lead a good life.

After she had been in charge of this monastery for many years, it pleased the merciful Author of our salvation that her holy soul be tested by a long infirmity of the body in order that, following the example of the apostle, her strength might be made perfect in weakness. She was afflicted with a fever that exhausted her with its burning heat, and for six years continuously she suffered from it without respite; yet in all that time she never ceased to give thanks to her Maker or to teach, in public and in private, the flock entrusted to her. Taught by her own example, she warned them all that when in bodily health they should serve the Lord in obedience, and when in adversity or sickness always give thanks to the Lord in faithfulness. In the seventh year of her sickness she had begun to suffer internal pain, and came to her last day. About cock-crow she received the viaticum of the holy communion, and then summoned the handmaids of Christ who were in the monastery to urge them to keep the peace of the Gospel with each other, and indeed with all the world; and while she was exhorting them she joyfully met her death, or rather, in the words of the Lord, she passed from death to life.

That same night it pleased Almighty God to make known her death by a vision in another monastery some distance away, called Hacanos, which she had built the same year. In this monastery there was a nun named Begu, who for more than thirty years had been vowed to chastity and served the Lord in the

monastic life. On this occasion she was resting in the sisters'
dormitory when she suddenly heard in the air the familiar
sound of the bell which used to rouse them for prayers and call
them together when one of them had been summoned from the
world. Opening her eyes, as she thought, she saw that the roof
of the house had been removed and all was filled with light
flooding down from above; and while gazing intently into this
light she saw, in the light itself, the soul of God's servant Hild,
escorted by a company of angels, being borne to Heaven. Waking from her sleep she saw the other sisters resting round about
her, and realized that what she had seen had been revealed to
her in a dream or a vision. Rising at once in great terror she ran
to the sister who was in charge of the monastery at the time in
place of the abbess, and whose name was Frigyth, and with
streams of tears and deep sighs of regret announced that the
mother of them all, Abbess Hild, had now departed from the
world, and while she watched, in the midst of a great light and
escorted by angels, had ascended to the abode of eternal light to
join the citizens of Heaven. When Frigyth heard this, she roused
all the sisters, summoned them to the church, and ordered them
to pray and sing psalms for the soul of their mother. They did
this assiduously for the remainder of the night, and at first light
there arrived brothers from the place where she died, to an-
nounce her death. They replied that they already knew of it, and
when they explained in detail how and when they had learned
the news it was found that her death had been revealed to them
in a vision at the same hour as the brothers reported that she
had departed from the world. So by a beautiful conjunction of
events God brought it about that while some witnessed her
departure from this life, others at the same time watched her
entry into the everlasting life of the spirit. These monasteries,
moreover, are almost thirteen miles apart.

They also say that on the same night, and in the same monastery where God's servant died, her death was revealed in a
vision to one of the virgins dedicated to God, who had an especial love for her. She saw her soul going to Heaven with the
angels, and at the very hour when it occurred gave a clear
account to the servants of Christ who were with her, and roused

them to pray for her soul even before the rest of the community learned of her death. It was early next morning when the others assembled and were told what had happened, as this nun was at the time living separately with some others in the furthest part of the monastery, where women who had recently entered the monastic life used to serve their probation until they were instructed in the Rule and admitted into the fellowship of the community.

✛

In her monastery there is a brother
to whom God has granted the gift of poetry

*Ecclesiastical
History of the
English People*
Book IV
Chapter 24

In the monastery of this abbess there was a brother specially favoured by the grace of God in that he used to compose songs on religious and devotional themes. Whatever of the holy scriptures he learned through interpreters he would render in a short time in his own, that is the English, tongue, in a most melodious and moving poetic diction. There were many whose hearts were inspired by his songs to despise the world and seek after the life of Heaven. Indeed, there were others after him among the English who set themselves to composing religious poems, but none could rival him. For he did not learn the art of poetry by instruction from men nor through a man, but received his poetic powers as a free gift by the favour of God. He was never able, therefore, to compose frivolous or trivial poetry: only devotional themes were suited to his devout style of utterance. Until well advanced in years he had lived in the secular habit, and had never learned any songs; and often at a feast, when it was decided that all the guests should sing one after another to provide entertainment, he used to get up in the middle of the meal when he saw the harp approaching him, and would go out and return to his own home.

On one occasion when he did this, he left the house where the feast was and went out to the stalls of the draught animals, as it was his turn to guard them that night. In due time he had settled down to sleep there, when in a dream someone stood beside him, who greeted him and called him by his name: 'Caedmon,' he said, 'sing something to me.'

He replied: 'I don't know how to sing; this was why I left the feast and came out here, because I could not sing.' Again the one who spoke to him said: 'Yet you must sing me something.'

'What should I sing?' he asked. He said: 'Sing of the beginning of Creation.' Hearing this reply, Caedmon at once began to sing in praise of God the Creator verses which he had never heard before, and whose sense is as follows:

> Now we must praise the Maker of the Kingdom of Heaven, the power of the Creator and His wisdom, the deeds of the Father of glory; how, since He is God eternal, He was the Author of all wonders, and created first for the sons of men the Heaven for their roof, and next, almighty Guardian of mankind, the earth.

This is the sense, but not the actual order of the words that he sang in his sleep; for poems, however well composed, cannot be translated word for word from one language into another without losing some of their beauty and dignity. When he arose, he remembered everything that he had sung in his sleep, and later added to it more verses in the same manner, singing God's praise in fitting style.

In the morning he came to his superior the reeve and told him of the gift he had received. He was then taken to the abbess and ordered to describe his dream to a large company of the more learned men and to recite his poem, so that they might all give an opinion as to the nature and origin of the gift of which he spoke. They all agreed that heavenly grace had been granted him by the Lord. They then explained to him a passage of sacred history or doctrine, bidding him, if he could, render it in poetic form. He undertook the task and went away, and when he returned in the morning he turned the prescribed passage into excellent verse. The abbess, therefore, recognizing God's grace in the man, instructed him to abandon the secular habit and take monastic vows, and with all her community she received him into the monastery and introduced him into the fellowship of the brothers, giving orders that he be taught the course of sacred history. Caedmon stored in his memory everything that he could learn by listening to them, like a clean animal chewing cud, and turned it into the sweetest poetry, and by his more melodious utterance made his teachers become in turn his audience. He sang of the creation of the world, the origin of the human race, and the whole story of Genesis; of the departure of Israel from Egypt and the entry into the promised land, and of many other stories from the holy scriptures; of the incarnation, passion and resurrection of the Lord, and His ascension into Heaven; and of the coming of the Holy Spirit, and the teaching of the apostles. He also made many poems about the terrors of the coming Judgement, the horrors of punishment in Hell, and the joys of the Kingdom of Heaven; and many others too, about God's mercies and judgements, in all of which he took care to draw men away from the love of sin and inspire them to take delight in the practice of good works. For he was a most devout man, humbly obedient to the discipline of the Rule, and in rebuking those who wished to act otherwise he displayed a burning zeal; and so it was that his life came to a beautiful end.

When the hour of his death was approaching, his body became weak during his last fourteen days, but the affliction was not so severe as to prevent him talking or walking at any time. Nearby there was a house into which they used to take those who were seriously ill and those who seemed near to death. So as evening fell, on the night on which he was to depart from the world, he asked his attendant to prepare in this house a place for him to rest; and the attendant, though wondering why he asked for this, when he seemed by no means likely to die, did as he had said. After taking their places there they talked and joked in good spirits with each of the other occupants in turn until after midnight, when Caedmon asked if they had the Eucharist in the house. They replied: 'What need have you of the Eucharist? You are not due to die yet but talk with us as cheerfully as if you were in good health.' Again he said: 'Yet bring me the Eucharist.' Taking it in his hand, he asked if their hearts were all at peace with him, and they had no complaint, quarrel or ill-feeling towards him. They all replied that their hearts were entirely at peace with him and quite without anger, and they asked him in turn to be at peace with them in his heart. He quickly replied: 'My heart is at peace, little children, with all God's servants.' And so he strengthened himself with the heavenly viaticum and prepared to enter the next life; and he enquired how near was the hour at which the brothers had to awake to sing their nightly praises to the Lord. They replied: 'It will not be long.' 'Good,' he said, 'then let us wait for that hour.' Signing himself with the sign of the holy cross he laid his head on the pillow, slept for a while, and so ended his life in silence. Thus it came about that, just as he had served God with a simple and pure heart and quiet devotion, so by a quiet death he left the world to come into His presence; and that tongue, which had uttered so many inspiring verses in praise of the Creator, uttered its last words, too, in His praise, as he made the sign of the cross and commended his spirit into God's hands. It seems also, from the events we have related, that he had foreknowledge of his death.

Cuthbert of Lindisfarne

The hermit bishop of Lindisfarne who became the great saint of the north country seems to lie at the very heart of Bede's *Historia*. Bede was fourteen when Cuthbert died on Inner Farne and he must have met and spoken with many who knew Cuthbert well.

When he wrote his prose *Life of Cuthbert* (see p.130), Bede had submitted his work for the scrutiny and approval of the Lindisfarne community and very probably made the journey up the coastline to bring his book in person. His detailed references to the island hermitage clearly suggest that he made the crossing to Inner Farne to see for himself the site where Cuthbert's life had drawn to its close, and he would surely have heard of the great work in progress, as the Lindisfarne Gospels were written and illuminated in the years after Cuthbert.

Bede's chronicles of Cuthbert were largely responsible for the fast-growing legend of the patron saint of the north. Apart from the anonymous *Life of Cuthbert* written by a monk of Lindisfarne, which provided his major primary source, the hagiography of Cuthbert is predominantly the work of Bede. In addition to the several chapters on Cuthbert's episcopacy in the *Historia*, all of which follow here, Bede had written no less than two earlier lives of the saint, a metrical *Life* and the prose *Life*. Even while Bede was writing these, Cuthbert lay entombed on Lindisfarne and pilgrims were already making their way across the sands between tides to pay homage and — in many recorded cases — to find miraculous healing at his shrine.

Bede was a young monk in his mid-twenties when, eleven years to the day after Cuthbert's death, the body was disinterred and found to be incorrupt. It is likely that the miniature Gospel of St John — certainly a product of the scriptorium of Wearmouth/Jarrow and known now as the Stonyhurst Gospel — was placed in a fold of Cuthbert's robe, probably as a tribute from the brothers of Bede's monastery, when the body was re-buried.

The post-mortal history of Cuthbert is quite as extraordinary as his life itself. Bede had been dead for more than half a century when the dragon prows of the Viking longships appeared off the Northumbrian coast and 'the fury of the northmen' was first visited on Lindisfarne. The pressure of Viking conquest forced the monks to abandon their island and move inland in search of greater safety. With them, as they journeyed around the north, up to the Firth of Forth and as far west as the Solway, they carried the body of their saint in its splendidly carved coffin of wood and the great gospel book of Lindisfarne.

The monks settled eventually at Chester-le-Street, where Cuthbert's remains lay for a hundred years. By this time the Viking raiders had become settlers and the rising pressure of the Viking kingdoms in the north forced the Lindisfarne community to move on once again. They settled at Ripon for a few months and then turned back towards Chester-le-Street, but Cuthbert's coffin refused to be drawn in that direction, seeming to call them towards the Wear and to a natural fortress of land almost surrounded by that river. There they stayed to build their church over the new tomb of their saint and there in the great cathedral of Durham —- 'half church of God, half castle 'gainst the Scot' as Sir Walter Scott later described it — the shrine of Cuthbert has stood for a thousand years.

Both during his life and afterwards, Cuthbert travelled widely through the north country, but his spirit seems most surely present today on the islands where he made his home and in the cathedral that houses the dark stone slab that bears the single name 'Cuthbertus' ...

CUTHBERT, A MAN OF GOD, BECOMES BISHOP;
HIS EARLIER LIFE AND TEACHING AS A MONK

In the same year in which King Egfrith met his death, as I have said, he had Cuthbert, a holy and venerable man, consecrated bishop of Lindisfarne. Cuthbert for many years had been living a solitary life, his body and mind subjected to the strictest discipline, on a small island called Farne, which lies out in the Ocean about nine miles from the church of Lindisfarne. From his earliest boyhood he had always felt a keen interest in the religious life, and when a youth he at once took the name and habit of a monk. At first he entered the monastery of Mailros, on the bank of the river Tweed, which was then ruled over by Abbot Eata, the gentlest and simplest of men, who later became bishop of Hagustaldesea, or rather of Lindisfarne. The prior of Mailros at that time was Boisil, a priest of the most virtuous character and endowed with the spirit of prophecy. Cuthbert

Ecclesiastical History of the English People Book IV Chapter 27

humbly submitted himself to Boisil's teaching, and learned from him both knowledge of the scriptures and examples of good works.

After Boisil departed to the Lord, Cuthbert was made prior of this monastery, and instructed many in the life under a Rule by the authority of his teaching and the example of his life. Not only did he give those in the monastery instruction in the life of the Rule and at the same time an example to follow, but he also sought to convert the neighbouring people far and wide from a life of foolish custom to the love of the joys of Heaven. For there were many who profaned the faith which they held by wicked deeds, and some also who in a time of plague neglected the mysteries of the faith into which they had been initiated, and had recourse to the false remedies of idolatry, as if they could ward off an affliction sent by God their creator with incantations, amulets or any other mysteries of devilish art. So to correct the errors of those who sinned in both these ways, he frequently left the monastery, sometimes on horseback, but more often on foot, and visited the neighbouring villages, preaching the way of truth to those who had gone astray; this had also been the practice of Boisil when he was prior. For at that time it was the custom of the English peoples, when a cleric or priest came to their village, to congregate together at his command to hear the Word; to listen gladly to what he said; and to carry out even more gladly what they could hear and understand. Cuthbert was so accomplished a speaker, so eager to convince them of his message, his face shining like an angel's, that none of his audience dared to hide from him the secrets of their hearts; all made open confession of their deeds, thinking it impossible that they should remain hidden from him, and they cleansed themselves of the sins they had confessed, as he ordered, by fruits worthy of repentance. It was his custom to travel and preach particularly in those remote districts and villages which were situated in high and rugged mountains; others shrank from visiting these places, and their poverty and ignorance deterred teachers from approaching them. Cuthbert, however, gladly undertook the good work, and toiled so patiently to bring them the benefit of his expert teaching that after leaving the monastery he was often away for a whole week, sometimes two or three, and occasionally even a full month, before returning home. He used to stay among the mountain people, calling the ignorant peasants to the ways of Heaven by his preaching and good works.

God's venerable servant had now spent many years in the monastery of Mailros and become renowned for his miraculous powers, when he was transferred by Eata, the monastery's most reverend abbot, to the island of Lindisfarne, in order that there also he might teach the brothers to keep the discipline of the Rule, both by his authority as prior and by the example of his own conduct. At that time this place, too, was governed by the reverend father Eata as abbot. From early times it was the custom there for the bishop to live with his clergy and the abbot with his monks, although they too belonged to the bishop's household. This was because Aidan, who was the first bishop of that place, came there with his monks and as a monk himself and established the monastic life there. Blessed Father Augustine is known to have done this still earlier in Kent, when the most reverend Pope Gregory wrote to him the words I quoted above: 'You, my brother, being trained in the monastic rules, ought not to live apart from your clergy, but should establish in the English church, lately brought to the faith by God's help, this way of life which at the Church's birth was followed by our forefathers; none of whom said that anything he possessed was his own, but they had all things in common.'

CUTHBERT, WHEN LIVING AS A HERMIT, BRINGS FORTH A SPRING
FROM THE DRY LAND BY THE POWER OF PRAYER, AND PRODUCES A CROP
FROM SEED SOWN BY HIS HANDS OUTSIDE THE SOWING SEASON

Later Cuthbert, his conduct inspired by ever more intense religious devotion, entered upon the contemplative life of the hermit in silent retreat from the world, as I have said. However, as I wrote at sufficient length some years ago about his life and virtues, both in heroic verses and in prose, for the present it will be enough simply to mention what he declared to the brothers

Ecclesiastical History of the English People Book IV Chapter 28

before going to the island: 'If by God's grace I am allowed to live in that place by the work of my own hands, I shall gladly stay there; but if not, I shall return to you directly, God willing.' Now it was a place utterly barren of water, corn and trees, and unsuitable besides for human habitation because frequented by evil spirits; but in accordance with the man of God's wish it became in all respects habitable, for at his arrival the evil spirits withdrew. After driving out these enemies he built for himself on the island with the help of the brothers a small dwelling, containing only the essential buildings, an oratory and a communal living-room surrounded by an earthwork. He ordered the brothers to dig a well in the floor of this living-room, although the ground was very hard and stony and there seemed no hope at all that a spring would be found there. When they carried out his order, in answer to the faith and prayers of God's servant it was found the next day to be full of water, and it still provides an ample supply of its heavenly bounty for all who visit there. He also asked for farming implements and wheat to be brought to him, but although he had prepared the ground and sowed it at the right time, by summer not a single ear or even blade had grown from the seed. So when the brothers made one of their customary visits he ordered barley to be brought, in case the nature of the soil or the will of God the bountiful required rather that a crop of that kind should grow there. This was brought to him quite outside the sowing season when there was no likelihood that it would bear a crop, but he sowed it in the same land, and before long a generous crop sprang up and supplied the man of God with the food he needed as the fruit of his own toil.

He served God there in solitude for many years, and the earthwork which enclosed his dwelling was so high that all he could see from it was the heaven that he longed to enter. It then came about that a large synod was assembled, in the presence of King Egfrith, near the river Aln at a place called Ad Tuifyrdi, meaning the two fords. Archbishop Theodore of blessed memory presided over the synod, and it was agreed unanimously that Cuthbert be elected to the bishopric of the church of Lindisfarne; but although many messengers and letters were sent to him it

'Sing of the beginning of Creation ...'

Caedmon's hymn from the 'Leningrad Bede,' written in the hand of one of the four scribes responsible for the manuscript who might possibly have been Bede himself.

M.E. Saltykov-Schedrin Public Library, St Petersburg: MS lat Q.v.I.18, f.107r

prouectioris aetatis consti
tutur. nil carminum aliquando
didicerat. unde non numquam
in conuiuio cum essel laetitiae
causa decretum. ut omnes
per ordinem cantare deberent.
ille ubi adpropinquare sibi
citharam cernebat. surgebat
a media cena. & egressus ad suam
domum repedabat. quod dum
tempore quodam faceret.
& relicta domu conuiuii.
egressus esset adstabula
iumentorum. quorum ei
custodia nocte illa erat
delegata. Ibiq; hora compe
tenti membra dedisset sopori.
adstitit ei quidam per somniu.
eumque salutans. ac suo
appellans nomine. Cædmon
inquit. canta mihi aliquid.
at ille respondit. Nescio
inquit cantare. nam & ideo
de conuiuio egressus huc
recessi. non poteram. quia cantare.
rursum ille qui cum eo loque
batur. Attamen ait

mihi cantare habes. quid
inquit debeo cantare.
& ille. canta inquit. principium
creaturarum. quo accepto
responso. statim ipse coepit
cantare in laudem di conditoris
uersus. quos numquam audierat.
quorum iste est sensus.
nunc laudare debemus auctore
regni caelestis. potentiam crea
toris. & consilium illius. facta
patris gloriae. quomodo ille
cum sit aeternus ds. omnium
miraculorum auctor exstitit.
qui primo filiis hominum
caelum pro culmine tecti.
dehinc terram custos humani
generis omnipotens creauit.
hic est sensus. non autem ordo
ipse uerborum. quae dormiens
ille canebat. neque enim
possunt carmina. quamuis
optime composita. ex alia
in aliam linguam. ad uerbum
sine detrimento sui decoris.
ac dignitatis transferri.
Exsurgens autem a somno

Nu scilun herga hefenricaes uard metudæs mehti and his modgithanc uerc uuldurfadur sue he uundra
gihuaes eci dryctin or astelidæ he aerist scop aelda barnum heben til hrofe haleg sceppend
tha middingard moncynnæs uard eci dryctin æfter tiadæ firum foldu frea allmehtig.

was impossible to prise him out of his monastery. At length
King Egfrith himself sailed to the island, accompanied by the
most holy Bishop Trumwin and other devout and powerful men.
From the island of Lindisfarne, too, many of the brothers gathered for the same purpose, and they all knelt and adjured him in
the name of the Lord, entreating him with many tears until they
drew him out, also in tears, from his sweet hiding-place and
dragged him to the synod. When he arrived there, he bowed
with great reluctance to their unanimous wish, and was compelled to submit his neck to the yoke of the office of bishop. He
was particularly prevailed on by the words of God's servant
Boisil, who revealed to him with prophetic insight everything
that would happen to him, and had foretold that he would be a
bishop. However, his consecration was not arranged at once, but
was held after the winter, which was just beginning. It took
place at Eboracum in the presence of King Egfrith at the festival
of Easter, and was attended by seven bishops, of whom the chief
was Theodore of blessed memory. At first, Cuthbert was elected
to the bishopric of the church of Hagustaldesea in place of
Tundbert, who had been deposed from the episcopate; but as his
own preference was to be put in charge of the church of Lindisfarne, in which he had lived, it was decided that Eata should
return to the church of Hagustaldesea, to which he had originally been appointed, and Cuthbert take charge of the church of
Lindisfarne.

Once consecrated, Cuthbert followed the example of the
blessed apostles in lending dignity to the order of bishop by his
virtuous works. He protected the people entrusted to him by
constant prayer, and called them to the things of Heaven by the
sound guidance that he gave. He followed a principle of particular value to teachers by first showing them by his own
actions what he taught them to do. He was above all else fired
with the love of God, patient and forbearing, devoutly dedicated
to the life of prayer, and friendly to all who came to him for
comfort. He held that it was a form of prayer also to give the
weaker brothers the benefit of his encouragement, for he knew
that He who said 'Thou shalt love the Lord thy God,' also said
'Thou shalt love thy neighbour.' He was remarkable for his use

of abstinence as a means of penance, and through the grace of contrition he was always intent on the things of Heaven. When, for example, he offered the saving Victim as a sacrifice to God, he committed his prayers to the Lord not with raised voice but with tears welling up from the depths of his heart.

✛

CUTHBERT, NOW A BISHOP, PREDICTS HIS OWN IMMINENT DEATH TO HEREBERT THE ANCHORITE

After spending two years in the bishopric he went back to his island hermitage, as he had been warned by a divine oracle that the day of his death was now approaching, or rather his entry into that life which alone deserves the name of life. He himself with his customary candour revealed this at the time to certain people, but in somewhat obscure language which was only clearly understood later; to others, however, he revealed it openly.

Ecclesiastical History of the English People Book IV Chapter 29

Now there was a priest of venerable life named Herebert, who had long been bound to the man of God by the ties of spiritual friendship. He lived a solitary life on an island in that great lake which is the source of the river Derwent, and used to visit Cuthbert every year and listen to his lessons of eternal salvation. Hearing that Cuthbert had arrived in the city of Lugubalia, he came as usual with a desire to be ever more inflamed, by the help of his teaching, with longing for the things of Heaven. They inspired each other with intoxicating draughts of the life of Heaven, and in the course of this the bishop said: 'Remember, brother Herebert, whatever need you have, to ask it of me now and speak of it with me; for after we have parted we shall never again see each other in this world with the eyes of the flesh. For I am certain that the time of my release is at hand, and the laying aside of my earthly tabernacle will be very soon.'

Hearing this the anchorite fell at his feet with tears and sighs, saying, 'I beseech you in the Lord's name not to desert me, but to remember your most faithful companion and ask God in His mercy that, as we have served Him together on earth, so we

'Cuthbertus'

St Cuthbert's tomb in the Chapel of the Nine Altars, Durham Cathedral.

may pass to Heaven together to behold His grace. For you know that I have always sought to live by the commands of your lips, and that any wrong I have done through ignorance or weakness I have taken the same care to set right at once in accordance with your will and judgement.' The bishop prostrated himself in prayer, and at once, his spirit assured that he had obtained his request from the Lord, said: 'Rise up, my brother, and do not weep, but be full of joy, for the Lord in His mercy has granted our request.'

The truth of this promise and prophecy was confirmed by the outcome of events, because after they parted they never again saw each other in the flesh, but their souls left their bodies on one and the same day, the twentieth of March, and were soon united in the beatific vision and borne by ministering angels to the heavenly Kingdom. But Herebert was first wasted by a long illness; and we may believe that the Lord in His mercy decreed this in order that, if in any respect he had less worth than blessed Cuthbert, the pain and punishment of his long suffering might make up for it, and being made equal in grace to his intercessor he might be counted worthy to leave the body with him at one and the same time, and be received also into one and the same abode of eternal bliss.

The most reverend father died on the island of Farne. He had earnestly begged the brothers that he might be buried in the same place where he had for long fought for the Lord; but at last he yielded to their entreaties and agreed to be carried back to the island of Lindisfarne and buried in the church there. After this was done, the venerable Bishop Wilfrid held the bishopric of that church for a year until someone could be elected to be consecrated bishop to succeed Cuthbert.

Afterwards Eadbert was consecrated bishop, a man notable both for knowledge of the holy scriptures and for observance of the commands of Heaven, especially almsgiving; for every year, in accordance with the Law, he gave to the poor a tenth part not only of his beasts but of all his grain, fruit and even clothing.

✝

AFTER BEING BURIED FOR ELEVEN YEARS HIS BODY IS FOUND TO BE INCORRUPT; NOT LONG AFTER HIS SUCCESSOR AS BISHOP DEPARTS FROM THE WORLD

Ecclesiastical History of the English People Book IV Chapter 30

Wishing to make more widely known how gloriously the Lord's servant Cuthbert lived after death, whose illustrious life before death was revealed by many miraculous signs, the divine providence proposed to the brothers, eleven years after his burial, that they should raise his bones and rebury them in a new coffin on the same spot but above the floor, to receive the veneration they deserved. They expected to find only dry bones, the rest of the body having decayed by now and turned to dust, as is usual with the dead. They reported their decision to Eadbert, their bishop, and he agreed to the plan and ordered them to make sure to carry it out on the anniversary of his burial. They did so, and when they opened the tomb they found the body whole and intact, as if still alive, and as the joints were still flexible he appeared to be asleep rather than dead. All the garments, too, in which his body had been clothed, were not merely unsullied but marvellously bright and fresh as when they were new. The brothers were at once filled with alarm at the sight, and hurried to tell the bishop what they had found. He at the time was living in solitude at a place remote from the church and encircled at high tide by the waves of the sea. It was his custom every year to spend Lent here and also the forty days before the Lord's nativity, observing a period of strict abstinence, prayer and tearful penance; and his venerable predecessor Cuthbert, before going to Farne island, also withdrew here for a time to fight for the Lord.

They brought him also part of the clothing in which the saint's body had been wrapped, and he received the gifts with gratitude and listened gladly to their account of the miracle, kissing the very garments with deep emotion as if they were still wrapped round the father's body. 'Put fresh garments on his body,' he said, 'in place of these you have brought me, and replace it thus in the coffin which you have prepared. I know for

certain that the place which has been consecrated by so miraculous a sign of heavenly grace will not long remain empty; and
blessed is the man whom the Lord, the Author and Giver of all
blessings, shall judge worthy to be granted a resting-place there.'
The bishop spoke these and similar words with many tears and
a voice trembling with powerful feeling, and when he had
finished the brothers did as he had ordered, wrapping the body
in a new garment and replacing it in a new coffin above the
floor of the sanctuary.

Very soon after, Bishop Eadbert, beloved of God, was afflicted
by serious illness, his distressed condition growing worse by the
day, and in a short time, on the sixth of May, he too departed to
the Lord. They placed his body in the tomb of blessed Father
Cuthbert, and put over it the coffin in which they had laid
Cuthbert's incorrupt body. It is said that miracles of healing
often occurred at this place, bearing witness to the merits of
them both, some of which I once recorded in my Life of Cuthbert. In this history I have considered it appropriate to add
others which I have chanced to hear recently.

✛

A MAN IS CURED OF PARALYSIS AT HIS TOMB

There was in the same monastery a brother called Baduthegn,
who had served for a long time as guest master. He is still alive,
and all the brothers and all the guests who visited the monastery
testify that he was a man of great piety and devotion who carried out the duties assigned to him solely for the sake of his
heavenly reward. One day he had been washing in the sea the
blankets or coverings which he used in the guest house, and was
returning home, when on the way he had a sudden seizure and
fell to the ground, where he lay prostrate for some time before at
length struggling to his feet again. As he stood up he felt one
side of his body to be paralysed from head to foot, and he
reached home with the greatest difficulty, leaning on a stick.
The disease gradually became worse, and by nightfall he was
still more severely afflicted, so that he could scarcely get up by

*Ecclesiastical
History of the
English People
Book IV
Chapter 31*

himself and walk when day returned. Thus disabled, he conceived an excellent plan. He would go to the church as best he could, approach the tomb of the most reverend father Cuthbert, and kneeling in supplication pray God in His mercy either that he might be released from this disease, if this were to his good, or, if the divine providence required him to endure such suffering still longer, that he might bear the pain inflicted on him with patience and a quiet mind. So he did as he had determined, and entered the church supporting his feeble limbs with a stick; and prostrating himself before the body of the man of God he prayed with earnest devotion that by His help the Lord might look favourably on him. While praying he seemed to fall into a deep sleep, and, as he himself used to relate afterwards, he felt a great, broad hand touch the place on his head that pained him, and at the same time pass over all that part of his body that had been afflicted with the disease down to his feet; and the pain gradually disappeared and health returned to him. At this he at once awoke and stood up completely cured. Giving thanks to the Lord for his recovery, he told the brothers what had happened to him, and amid universal rejoicing returned to the duties that he performed so conscientiously, now tried and chastened as if by a scourge.

The garments also which had clothed Cuthbert's body, dedicated to God, before and after his death, themselves possessed the grace of healing, as anyone who reads the book of his life and miracles will discover.

'There is an island called Farne lying well out at sea ...'

Inner Farne from Monks' House.

From the
Life of Cuthbert

Bede's prose *Life of Cuthbert* was written around the year 721 in response to a request from the brothers of Lindisfarne, and its dedication is addressed to Bishop Eadfrith, the scribe of the Lindisfarne Gospels. Bede must have visited the island monastery at least once, probably to research his material at first hand and to present his finished work for the approval of the abbot and his community. Bede had written his metrical *Life of Cuthbert* some five years earlier and that work may well have suggested him to the Lindisfarne monks as the best-qualified biographer of their great saint.

The chapters from Bede's prose *Life of Cuthbert* that follow have been chosen to supplement the *Historia's* rather more formal biography.

'Cuthbert's Vision' is not included in the *Historia.* Bede tells how the young Cuthbert, watching his sheep at night on the Lammermuir Hills, had a vision of the ascension of Aidan and was thus inspired to enter the monastic life at Mailros, Old Melrose on the Tweed and not the site of the ruined border abbey.

'Cuthbert and the Otters' is Bede's version of one of the most famous Cuthbert wildlife stories. Bede draws on the eye-witness account of a monk of Coludesbyrig — Coldingham on the Berwickshire coast — who watched as Cuthbert immersed himself in the cold North Sea through a night of prayer and emerged to be dried by two otters. Otters are not commonly found on the North Sea coast today, but they were probably much more numerous in Cuthbert's time. Gavin Maxwell suggests in *Ring of Bright Water* that otters do indeed behave on occasions in the way Bede describes, although coming out of the sea with half a gallon of salt water in their fur they may not have been the most effective of beach towels.

Bede's chapters describing Cuthbert's life on Farne provide the vivid portrait of a holy man surrounded by seals and seabirds on his sea-girt outcrop of the Great Whin Sill, which has been the centre of Cuthbert's tradition down all the centuries. Finally, his evocative and moving account of the death of Cuthbert is quoted directly and at length from

Herefrith, one of the brothers who shared the saint's last hours and lit the torches that signalled his passing to the anxious watchers on Lindisfarne.

✛

IN THE COMPANY OF SHEPHERDS, HE SEES THE SOUL OF
THE HOLY BISHOP AIDAN BEING BORNE TO HEAVEN BY ANGELS

When Christ's grace, which guides the life of the faithful, determined that His servant should prove his worth in a stricter way of life, and earn the glory of a nobler reward, he happened to be keeping watch over the flocks entrusted to him far off in the mountains. One night while his companions slept he stayed awake, as usual, and was praying, when he suddenly saw a stream of light from the sky pierce the darkness of the long night, and in it choirs of the heavenly host come down to earth; and without delay they took with them a soul of great brightness, and returned to their home above. The youth beloved of God was deeply moved by this vision, and inspired to submit himself to the grace of spiritual discipline and to join that illustrious company of men whose reward is everlasting life and happiness. He at once gave praise and thanks to God, and also called his companions and encouraged them like a brother to praise God. 'How pitiful we are,' he said, 'given up to sleep and sloth, and unworthy to see the light enjoyed by Christ's ever watchful servants. I stayed awake at prayer for only a small part of the night, and look what great wonders I saw God perform. The gate of Heaven was opened, and the spirit of a saint was taken in there by a company of angels; and while we live in deepest darkness, he now beholds in everlasting bliss the glory of the heavenly abode and Christ its King. I am sure that he was some holy bishop or some man of renown from the number of the faithful, that I saw borne to Heaven in the splendour of that great light and escorted by so many bands of angels.' With these words Cuthbert, the Lord's man, fired the hearts of the shepherds to worship and praise God. When morning came, he

Life of Cuthbert
Chapter 4
Cuthbert's
vision

'I wrote at length about his life and virtues, both in heroic verses and in prose'

An illustrated page from a manuscript of the prose *Life of Cuthbert* produced, probably at Durham, in the early twelfth century shows Bede at work on his text and offering his finished book to the abbot and community on Lindisfarne.

Bodleian Library, Oxford: MS 16. 5. p.ii

'He had two buildings for his dwelling, an oratory and
another small habitation'

St Cuthbert's Chapel on Inner Farne, built in the fourteenth century on the traditional site of Cuthbert's hermitage.

learned that Aidan, bishop of the church of Lindisfarne and a man of outstanding virtue, had entered the Kingdom of Heaven at the very time when he had seen him taken from the body; and he at once delivered the flocks he was tending to their owners and decided to enter a monastery.

✣

ANIMALS OF THE SEA, IN WHICH HE SPENT THE NIGHT IN PRAYER, MINISTER TO HIM WHEN HE COMES OUT; AND A BROTHER WHO SAW THIS BECOMES SICK WITH FEAR, BUT IS RESTORED BY HIS PRAYERS

Life of Cuthbert
Chapter 10
Cuthbert and
the otters

The holy Cuthbert performed more and more signs and miracles in that monastery, and everywhere the fame of his works increased. There was a nun called Ebba, a mother of Christ's handmaids who was in charge of the monastery at a place named Coludesbyrig. She was by birth King Oswy's sister, and was honoured by everyone as much for her piety as her noble rank. She sent to the man of God, asking him to consent to visit her and her monastery for the purpose of exhortation. He could not refuse a request made in heartfelt love by God's handmaid, and so he came there and stayed for some days, revealing to them all the way of righteousness that he preached as much by his deeds as by his words. In his customary fashion he went out alone at night to pray while the others were at rest, and after keeping long vigil through the dead of night, he would at last return home at the very hour when they said the office together. One night one of the brothers of the monastery saw him going silently out, and secretly followed in his footsteps, seeking to discover where he was going and what his purpose was.

Leaving the monastery with the spy following, Cuthbert went down to the sea-shore beneath the monastery; and going deep into the water until the swelling waves rose up to his neck and arms, he spent the dark hours of the night watching and singing praises accompanied by the sound of the waves. When dawn approached he went on to the land and again began to pray, kneeling on the shore. As he did so, there at once came out from the depths of the sea two four-footed creatures which are commonly called otters. Stretching themselves out in front of him on the sand, they began to warm his feet with their breath and sought to dry him on their fur. Having performed their services, they received his blessing and slid back beneath the waves in which they lived. Cuthbert also soon returned home and sang the hymns of the office with the brothers at the proper hour. However, the brother who watched him from the cliffs became panic-stricken and could barely stagger home, such was the distress that gripped him. Early in the morning he went to Cuthbert and prostrated himself on the ground, begging him in tears to forgive his wicked and foolish presumption, as he was quite sure that Cuthbert knew what he had done that night and why he was distressed. Cuthbert said to him: 'What is wrong with you, brother? What have you done? Have you tried to follow and spy on my nightly journey? I will grant you pardon for what you have done only on this condition, that you promise to tell no one what you have seen until after my death.' In giving this command he followed the example of Him who, when He showed the glory of His majesty to the disciples on the mount, said: 'Tell the vision to no man until the Son of Man be risen again from the dead.' When the brother promised as commanded, he blessed him, and wiped away both his guilt and the distress that his rashness had brought on him. While Cuthbert was alive, the brother kept silent about the miracle he had seen, but after his death he made a point of telling it to many people.

✛

HE DRIVES OUT THE EVIL SPIRITS
AND BUILDS HIMSELF A DWELLING ON FARNE ISLAND

After completing a long period of years in that monastery he at last entered with great joy, and with the goodwill of his abbot and brothers, into the life of solitary retreat that he had long desired, sought and prayed for. He was glad that after the perfection of his long active life he was now judged worthy to rise to the peace of the contemplation of God. He rejoiced that

Life of Cuthbert
Chapter 17
Cuthbert on
Farne

'Cuddy's Ducks'

Eider on the Northumberland coast. These handsome, gentle residents of the
Farne Islands enjoy a long-standing association with St Cuthbert which has
earned them their local nickname of 'Cuddy's Ducks.'

OPPOSITE

*'His first attempt at the solitary life was to withdraw to a place which
offered greater seclusion in the outer precincts of the monastery'*

Hobthrush Island off Lindisfarne was the site of Cuthbert's first hermitage.

he was attaining to the condition of those of whom the psalmist sings, 'They shall go from strength to strength; the God of gods shall be seen in Sion.' His first attempt at the solitary life was to withdraw to a place which offered greater seclusion in the outer precincts of the monastery; but after spending some time there in solitude, fighting his invisible enemy with prayer and fasting, he finally sought a place of combat more distant and more remote from mankind, to set himself a still greater challenge. There is an island called Farne lying well out at sea. It is not like Lindisfarne, which twice a day becomes an island with the rising of the Ocean tide, called 'rheuma' in Greek, but becomes joined to the mainland again when the ebb of the tide exposes its shores. Farne lies several miles to the south-east of this half-island, and is surrounded by the Ocean, very deep on its landward side and on its further side boundless. No one before the Lord's servant Cuthbert had been able to live alone on this island without trouble, as it was haunted by evil spirits; but when the soldier of Christ entered there, armed with the helmet of salvation, the shield of faith, and the sword of the spirit which is the word of God, all the fiery darts of the wicked one were quenched, and the wicked foe himself, together with the whole crowd of his allies, was driven far away. This soldier of Christ, having routed the army of the usurpers and become monarch of the land he had entered, founded a city worthy of his power and built within it houses similarly in keeping with his city. It is a structure almost circular in plan, measuring about four to five poles from wall to wall. On the outside the wall itself is higher than a man standing upright; but on the inside he made it much higher by cutting away the rocky ground, so that he could see nothing except the sky from his dwelling, to protect his holy life against tempting sights or thoughts and raise the whole tenor of his mind above earthly desires. He made this wall not of cut stone or bricks and mortar, but of merely unworked stones and turf that he had removed in excavating the middle of the enclosure. Some of these stones were so large that it hardly seemed possible that four men could have lifted them, yet with the help of angels he was found to have brought them there from elsewhere and put them on the wall. He had two buildings in his dwelling, an oratory and another small habita-tion suitable for the ordinary business of life. He completed their walls by digging or cutting away a quantity of earth inside and outside, and he roofed them with rough-hewn timber and straw. Away at the island's landing-place there was a larger house where brothers coming to visit him could be received and rest, and not far from it there was a well for their use.

HE PRODUCES WATER FROM THE DRY GROUND BY PRAYER; HIS LIFE AS A HERMIT

Now his dwelling had no water, being built on very hard and almost solid rock. The man of God had not yet shut himself away from the sight of visitors, and so he summoned the broth-ers and said: 'You see that the dwelling I have occupied lacks a well; but I pray you, let us ask Him who turns the solid rock into a standing water and the flint into fountains of waters, to vouchsafe to open up for us a spring of water even from this stony rock, giving glory not unto us but unto His name. Let us dig in the middle of my little dwelling, and I believe that He will make us drink from the river of His pleasures.' So they dug a pit, and found it the next morning filled with water welling up from below. There was no doubt that it was through the man of God's prayers that this water had been drawn from ground which had previously been utterly dry and hard. Strangely enough, the water kept within the limits of its original channel, never bubbling over to flood the floor or failing through being drawn off; it was so regulated by the grace of God the bountiful that it never exceeded its user's needs nor failed to supply his needs.

Life of Cuthbert
Chapter 18

So after making a dwelling with the buildings mentioned, assisted by the brothers, Cuthbert the man of God began to live in solitude, although at first when visited by the brothers he would come out from his cell and minister to them. When he had devoutly washed their feet in warm water, they sometimes made him take off his shoes also and allow them to wash his

'No one before Cuthbert had been able to live alone on this island without trouble, as it was haunted by evil spirits'

Shags on Staple Island to the east of Inner Farne. The strangely sinister aspect of these birds may well have suggested 'evil spirits' to the Anglo-Saxon imagination.

'Not only did the creatures of the air minister to the venerable man, but so too did sea animals ...'

Atlantic Grey Seals on the Farne Islands. These 'people of the sea' — as they are called by the Irish — would have been Cuthbert's closest neighbours on his island hermitage.

feet, as he had so far lifted his mind above the care of the body and applied it exclusively to the care of his soul that, once he had put on the leather boots that he used, he would wear them for months at a time. Let it be said also that he sometimes put his boots on at Easter and did not remove them until the return of Easter the following year, and then only for the washing of the feet which takes place on the day of the Lord's Supper. As a result of kneeling frequently to pray while wearing his boots he was found to have a long, thick callus at the junction of his feet and shins. Later, as his desire for perfection increased, he remained shut up in his hermitage, withdrawn from the sight of men, and learned to live a solitary life of fasting, prayer and vigil, rarely conversing from inside with visitors, and that only through a window. At first he opened this and was glad to be seen by the brothers and to see the brothers with whom he spoke; but as time passed he even closed the window, and opened it only to give a blessing or for some other definite need.

With a word he drives birds away from the crops that he has sown with his own hand

Life of Cuthbert
Chapter 19

At first he received from them a little bread to eat, and drank from his own well; but later, following the example of the fathers, he considered it more fitting to live by the labour of his own hands. He therefore asked for tools to be brought to him with which to work the ground, and some wheat to sow. But though the land was sown in springtime it produced no crop up to midsummer. So when the brothers made him one of their customary visits, the man of God said to them: 'It may be that either the character of this ground or the will of God is against my growing wheat here. I pray you, bring some barley, to see if that can produce a crop. If God does not wish to grant increase to that, it is better for me to return to the monastery than to be supported here by the labour of others.' When the barley was brought he put it in the ground long after the sowing season when there was no prospect of a harvest, yet it soon sprang up in abundance and produced a plentiful crop. When it began to ripen, birds came and eagerly set about eating it up. Christ's most devout servant approached them; and he afterwards described what happened himself, as he was a man of cheerful demeanour and friendly personality who would often make known some of the blessings that he had gained by his faith, in order to strengthen the faith of his listeners.

'Why,' he said, 'do you touch crops that you did not sow? Do you perhaps have more need of them than I? If you have been given permission by God, do what He has allowed; but if not, be gone and do no further damage to what does not belong to you.'

These were his words, and at the first sound of his command the whole flock of birds departed and refrained ever afterwards from attacking those crops. And on this occasion also the two miracles performed by Christ's venerable servant resembled the acts of two of the fathers. In drawing water from the rock he followed the blessed father Benedict, who is said to have performed an almost identical miracle in the same way, though producing a more plentiful supply as there were more people suffering from the lack of water. And again, in driving away the birds from the crops he followed the example of the most reverend and holy father Anthony, who with a single rebuke restrained wild asses from damaging a little garden that he had planted himself.

✛

THE RAVENS, BY PRAYERS AND A GIFT,
ATONE FOR THE WRONG THEY HAVE DONE TO THE MAN OF GOD

I should like to tell also of a miracle performed by blessed Cuthbert after the example of the same father Benedict, in which the stubborn pride of men is plainly put to shame by the humble obedience of birds. There were some ravens that had for a long time made that island their home. One day, when they were building their nest, the man of God saw them tear with their beaks the little guest house for the brothers which I mentioned

Life of Cuthbert
Chapter 20

above, remove the straw with which it was thatched and carry it off to use for their nest. He stopped them with a slight gesture of his right hand, and ordered them to cause no more harm to the brothers. When they scorned his command, he said: 'In the name of Jesus Christ, be gone at once; do not dare to remain any longer in the place you are damaging.' Scarcely had he finished speaking when they went sadly away. After three days one of the pair returned, and finding Christ's servant digging, it spread its wings in sorrow, bowed its head to its feet, and humbly begged his forgiveness, expressing its meaning as best it could. The venerable father understood, and gave it permission to return; and having got leave to come back it at once went off to fetch its mate. Without delay they both returned, each bearing the fitting gift of a piece of hog's lard. Afterwards, when the brothers visited him, the man of God would often show them the lard and offer it for greasing their shoes, calling on them to recognize what great regard men should have for obedience and humility when a proud bird had made haste, by prayers, contrition and gifts, to atone for the wrong it had done to a man of God. And indeed, to give men an example of amendment of life, they stayed for many years afterwards on that island and made their nest, never presuming to trouble anyone. No one should find it absurd to learn a lesson in virtue from birds, as Solomon says, 'Go to the ant, thou sluggard, consider her ways and be wise.'

✛

EVEN THE SEA SERVES HIS NEEDS

Life of Cuthbert
Chapter 21

Not only did the creatures of the air minister to the venerable man, but so too did sea animals and indeed the sea itself. For if a man serves the Author of all creation faithfully and with all his heart, it is no wonder that every creature should defer to his commands and wishes. Yet we in general lose control of the creation that is subject to us because we neglect to do service in our turn to the Lord and Creator of all things. The very sea, as I say, was quick to minister to Christ's servant when he had need.

He was intending to build himself a hut in his hermitage, very small but fit for his daily needs. On the side facing the sea the rock had been hollowed out by the regular washing of the tides, making a cleft very deep and quite wide; and to bridge this cleft a support twelve feet long was needed. So he asked the brothers who had come to visit him to bring him on their return some wood twelve feet long to make the support for his little house. They promised that they would do as he asked very gladly; but after receiving his blessing and returning home, they forgot the father's request and returned on the appointed day without bringing the wood they were asked for.

Receiving them with great kindness and commending them to God with his usual prayer, he said: 'Where is the wood that I asked you to bring?' At this they remembered his request, confessed that they had forgotten, and begged his forgiveness for their error. The man dealt very gently with them, speaking some kind words of comfort and bidding them stay on the island and rest until morning. 'I believe,' he said, 'that God will not forget my wish and my need.' They did as he had said, and when they rose in the morning they saw that the night tide had brought in some wood of the required length and left it on the very spot over which it was to be laid to support the building. When they saw it, they at once wondered at the holiness of the venerable man to whom even the elements did service; and with a proper sense of shame they condemned their own slackness of mind, for needing even the unfeeling element to teach them what obedience is due to saints.

IN SICKNESS HE ENDURES GREAT TEMPTATIONS,
AND GIVES INSTRUCTIONS CONCERNING HIS BURIAL WHEN ABOUT TO DIE

Cuthbert the man of God made again for his island home as soon as the feast of the Lord's nativity was over. As he was about to board his boat, a crowd of the brothers stood round him and one of them, an old monk of venerable life, strong in faith but now weakened in body by dysentery, asked him: 'Tell

Life of Cuthbert
Chapter 37
The death of
Cuthbert

us, lord bishop, when we may hope for your return.' To this simple question he gave a simple reply in turn, as he knew the truth: 'When you bring my body back here.' For almost two months he experienced the joy of returning to his life of peace, and subjected his body and mind to the rigour of his strict routine; but then he was attacked by a sudden illness, and began to be made ready by the fire of earthly pain for the joys of everlasting bliss. I shall describe his death in the words of the man who gave me an account of it, a devoutly religious priest named Herefrith, who at the time was abbot in charge of the monastery of Lindisfarne.

'After being wasted by three weeks of continuous sickness,' he said, 'he came to his end like this. His illness began on a Wednesday, and again on a Wednesday when it had run its course he departed to the Lord. I had gone to the island with the brothers three days before the sickness began, wishing as usual to receive the comfort of his blessing and counsel. On the morning when he first became ill, I went to him, giving the usual signal of my approach, and he came to the window and gave a sigh in response to my greeting. I said to him, "What is wrong with you, my lord bishop? Did you have an attack of your sickness last night?"

'"Yes," he said, "I had an attack of sickness last night." I thought that he was speaking of his old complaint which used to trouble him almost every day, and not of a new and unfamiliar affliction. Without asking more, I said, "Give us your blessing, as the time has now come for us to set sail and return home."

'"Do as you say," he replied. "Board your boat and return home safely. And when God takes my soul to Himself, bury me in this dwelling close to the south side of my oratory and to the east of the holy cross which I have erected there. On the north side of the oratory there is a sarcophagus hidden under the turf, which the venerable Abbot Cudda once gave me. Lay my body in it, wrapped in the linen cloth which you will find there. I was unwilling to wear it while I lived, but for love of a woman beloved of God, Abbess Verca, who sent it to me, I have taken care to keep it to wrap my body in."

'When I heard this I said, "I beg you, father, now that I hear you are sick and approaching death, allow some of the brothers to stay here and look after you." But he said, "Go now, and return at the proper time." I begged him earnestly to let a servant stay, but met with no success, and at length I asked him when we should return. "When God wills and makes His will clear to you," he said.

'We did as he commanded, and I at once summoned all the brothers into the church and told them to offer constant prayer for him. "For it seems to me," I said, "from some words of his, that the day is approaching when he will depart to the Lord." I was anxious about our return because of his illness, but for five days a storm prevented us from getting back. The outcome proved that this was a divine dispensation; for Almighty God, to chasten and cleanse His servant of every stain of earthly weakness, and to show his enemies that they were powerless against the strength of his faith, wished him to be cut off from mankind for that period of time and put to the test of bodily pain and a keener combat with the ancient foe.

'When calm weather was restored and we made for the island again, we found that he had left his hermitage and was sitting in the house where we used to stay. The brothers who had accompanied me were forced by some urgent business to sail back to the neighbouring shore, and so I remained on the island and at once set about ministering to the father. I warmed some water and washed his foot, which had for long been swollen and now had a suppurating ulcer on it which needed treatment. I also warmed some wine, which I brought and asked him to taste, as I could see by his face that he was exhausted by both lack of food and sickness.

'When I had finished attending to him he sat down again on the couch, and I sat beside him. As he was silent, I said, "I see, my lord bishop, that you have been greatly troubled by your illness since we left you, and I wonder why you refused to let us appoint some of the brothers to look after you when we went away."

'But he said, "It happened by the providence and will of God, that I might be deprived of human society and help and endure certain afflictions. For after you left me the sickness at once began to grow worse. My reason for leaving my dwelling and coming in here was so that any of you who came to look after me could find me here and not have to go into my dwelling. Since I came in and laid my limbs on this couch I have not moved from here, but remained for the last five days and nights resting here."

'I said to him, "And how could you live like this, my lord bishop? Have you gone all this time without taking food?" He then drew back the coverlet on which he was sitting and showed me five onions concealed there, and said, "This was my food for the last five days. Whenever my mouth grew so thirsty that it became dry and parched, I refreshed and cooled myself by tasting these." One of the onions was less than half chewed away. He added, "And my assailants have never harassed me so frequently in all the time since I began to live on this island as during the last five days."

'I did not dare to ask what the temptations were of which he spoke; I only asked him to let some of us wait upon him. He agreed, and kept some of us with him, including the elder Bede, a priest who was regularly in close attendance on him. It was because Bede had reliable knowledge of all the gifts he had given and received that the bishop particularly wanted him to stay with him, so that if he had received gifts from anyone without making a proper return, he could be reminded of it by Bede and before he died restore to each what was due to him. He also made a special request for one of the other brothers to be among his servants. This one had been seriously ill with diarrhoea for a long time, unable to be cured by the doctors, but by virtue of his devotion, good sense and dignity was a worthy witness of the man of God's last words and the manner of his departure to the Lord.

'Meanwhile I returned home and told the brothers that the venerable father had ordered that he should be buried on his own island. "It seems to me much more fitting and appropriate," I said, "that we should gain his permission for his body to be brought across here and buried with due honour in the church." They agreed with what I said, and we came and asked the bishop, saying, "We did not dare, lord bishop, to spurn your command that you be buried here, yet we thought it right to ask that we might have the honour to carry you across to our monastery and keep you with us."

'But he said, "It was my wish that my body should rest here where in a small way I have fought the fight for the Lord, where I desire to finish the course, and from where I hope to be raised up by a merciful Judge to receive the crown of righteousness. I also think it more convenient for you that I should rest here, because of the incursions of fugitives and malefactors of every kind. They are likely to take refuge by my body, because, unworthy as I am, the rumour has spread abroad that I am a servant of Christ; and you will very often have to intercede for them with the rulers of the world, and will find the presence of my body a great burden to you."

'But we pleaded with him for a long time, assuring him that a burden of that kind would be welcome to us and light to bear; and at last the man of God spoke words of counsel. "If you wish to override my plan," he said, "and take my body back there, it seems best to me that you should entomb it inside your church, so that you yourselves may visit my sepulchre when you wish, and it may be in your power to decide whether any visitors should approach it." Kneeling on the ground we thanked him for his permission and counsel, and returned home; and from that time we continued to visit him very frequently.'

✛

HE GIVES HIS LAST COMMANDS TO THE BROTHERS,
AND AFTER RECEIVING THE VIATICUM HE YIELDS UP HIS SPIRIT IN PRAYER

'I went in to him about the ninth hour of the day, and found him lying in a corner of his oratory opposite the altar. I sat down beside him. He said little, because the grave nature of his illness had made it difficult for him to speak. But when I urged him to say what advice and what last farewell he would leave as his testament to the brothers, he began a brief but forceful discourse on peace and humility, and on the need to beware of

Life of Cuthbert
Chapter 39

those who would rather fight against these things than take delight in them.

'"Always keep God's peace and love among yourselves," he said, "and when you have to take counsel about your affairs, take great care to be of one mind in your counsels. Live in mutual goodwill also with Christ's other servants, and do not despise those of the household of faith who come to you for hospitality, but see that you welcome them, give them lodging, and send them on their way with friendship and kindness. On no account must you think yourselves superior to those others who share your faith and way of life. But with those who stray from the unity of Catholic peace, by not celebrating Easter at the proper time or by evil living, you must have no communion. And I would have you know and remember that if necessity compels you to choose one of two evils, I would much prefer you to dig up my bones from the tomb and take them with you and leave this place, to dwell wherever God ordains, than that you should make any compromise with wickedness and bow your necks beneath the yoke of schismatics. Strive to learn and observe with the utmost care the Catholic statutes of the fathers, and practise assiduously those duties of the life of the Rule that God in His mercy has seen fit to give you through my ministry. For I know that even if I was despised by some while I lived, yet after my death you will see what I was and that my teaching is not to be despised."

'The man of God spoke these and similar words intermittently because the severity of his illness, as I have said, had restricted his power of speech. He spent a quiet day until evening, in expectation of the blessed state that was to come, and stayed awake also throughout the night in quiet prayer. But at the customary time of night prayer he received from me the sacraments of salvation and fortified his death, which he knew had now come, with the communion of the Lord's body and blood; and raising his eyes to Heaven and lifting up his outstretched hands, he released his soul, intent on God's praises, to the joys of the Kingdom of Heaven.

✛

IN ACCORDANCE WITH THE PROPHECY OF THE PSALM WHICH THEY SANG
AT HIS DEATH, THE BROTHERS OF LINDISFARNE ARE ATTACKED,
BUT DEFENDED WITH THE HELP OF THE LORD

'I at once went out and announced his death to the brothers, *Life of Cuthbert*
who had also passed the night in watching and prayer. At that Chapter 40
moment, according to the order of lauds, they were chanting the
fifty-ninth psalm, which begins, *O God, thou hast cast us off and*
hast broken us down; thou hast been angry, and hast had compassion
on us. Without delay one of them lit two candles, and holding
one in either hand went up to higher ground to show the brothers who were in the monastery of Lindisfarne that his holy soul
had now departed to the Lord. This was the way in which they
had agreed among themselves to signal the death of that holiest
of men.

Far away on the island of Lindisfarne, a brother had been
keeping watch and awaiting the hour of his death in a watch
tower facing towards Farne, and on seeing the signal he ran
quickly to the church, where the whole community of the brothers was assembled and singing the psalms of the night office. It
happened that as he entered they too were singing the psalm
mentioned above; and events showed that this was ordained by
divine providence. For after the man of God was buried, such
trials shook that church like a great gust of wind that many of
the brothers chose to leave the place rather than live among such
perils. A year later, however, Eadbert, a man of outstanding
virtues, with an excellent knowledge of the scriptures and a
strong dedication to works of charity, was consecrated to the
bishopric; and the storms that caused such havoc were dispelled.
To use the words of scripture, *The Lord did build up Jerusalem,*
that is, the vision of peace, *and gathered together the outcast of*
Israel. He healed the broken in heart and bound up their wounds, so
that they had plainly revealed to them the meaning of the psalm
that they were singing when they learned of the blessed man's
death. It signified that after his death the members of his community were to be cast off and broken down, but that after the

revelation of the wrath that threatened them they would be revived by the mercy of Heaven. The rest of this psalm is in harmony with this meaning, as anyone who studies it again will see. We placed the father's venerable body on the boat and took it back to the island of Lindisfarne. It was received by a large crowd that came to meet it and by chanting choirs, and was buried in a stone sarcophagus, in the church of the blessed apostle Peter on the right of the altar.'

'I at once went out and announced his death to the brothers. Without delay one of them lit two candles and went up to higher ground to show the brothers who were in the monastery of Lindisfarne that his holy soul had now departed to the Lord'

Inner Farne at dusk from Lindisfarne. The beam just visible from the Inner Farne light recalls the monk's signal on the night of Cuthbert's death.

John of Beverley

With the chapters on John — bishop of Hexham, archbishop of York and saint of Beverley — the *Historia* reaches the years of Bede's maturity. John had died in his own monastery at Beverley — Bede's In Derawuda or 'in the wood of the Deiri' — only ten years before Bede completed his history.

Bede's account was derived from first-hand sources, principally, it seems, from Berthun, John's successor at Beverley. In his concluding auto-biographical note Bede tells us that it was John, then bishop of Hexham, who ordained him first as deacon and later as priest at Jarrow. So the portrait we are offered here of this traditionally kindly man from Harpham-on-the-Wolds surely stems from Bede's immediate personal experience.

Like Wilfrid, his immediate contemporary, John was a graduate of Abbess Hild's dual foundation at Whitby. It was during Wilfrid's politically prompted exile on the continent that John succeeded Eata as bishop of Hexham. He became archbishop of York in 705, and it may well have been around that time — Bede is not specific on the date — that he founded his monastery at Beverley, almost certainly on the site of an earlier foundation. It was at Beverley that John spent his last years and there that he was buried in St Peter's Chapel. His tomb remains today in the nave of Beverley's medieval minster.

Bede's list of John's miracles of healing suggests that the saint possessed some measure of expertise in the medicine of his time, as is evident from his guidance on the therapeutic bleeding of the nun of Watton in accordance with the phases of moon and tide.

Traditionally St John, like Cuthbert, had a great affinity with animals. The chronicles of William of Malmesbury tell us that the aggression of the bulls and bulldogs in the medieval bullpit close to John's church at Beverley was miraculously quelled by the proximity of the saint's relics. There is also a local tradition that the waters of St John's Well at Harpham have the property of calming wild and savage beasts.

The last of John's miracles recorded by Bede tells of a horse race held by students accompanying the saint on his travels and John's premonition and healing of an injury to one of the young horsemen. Bede recalls how he learned of the miracle from the man himself, the priest Herebald.

In the light of Herebald's memoir, it is perhaps fitting that so famous a racecourse is to be found close by the great minster at Beverley on modern Humberside.

✛

BISHOP JOHN CURES A DUMB YOUTH BY HIS BLESSING

At the start of Aldfrith's reign Bishop Eata died, and John, a saintly man, took charge of the church of Hagustaldesea. Many miracles are told concerning John by people who knew him well, and particularly by his former deacon Berthun, a most venerable and truthful man, now abbot of the monastery of In Derawuda, meaning the wood of the Deiri. I have thought it appropriate to put on record some of these miracles.

Ecclesiastical History of the English People Book V Chapter 2

Not far from the church of Hagustaldesea, about a mile and a half in fact, and separated from it by the river Tyne, there is a house hidden away and surrounded by a sparse wood and an earthwork. It has an oratory of St Michael the Archangel, in which the man of God, when a favourable opportunity pre-sented itself, and especially during Lent, used very often to stay with a few companions and devote himself to quiet prayer and study. On one occasion at the beginning of Lent when he came to stay there, he asked his companions to look for a poor man burdened with some serious illness or in dire need, so that they could keep him with them during their stay to receive their charity, as was always his custom.

Now in a nearby village there was a dumb youth who was known to the bishop, as he had often visited him previously to receive alms. He had never been able to utter a single word, and his head was so scabby and covered with scurf that the crown of his head had always been completely bald, though encircled by a few bristling hairs. The bishop, therefore, ordered him to be fetched and a small hut made for him in the enclosure of the house, so that he could live there and receive alms from them each day. When one week of Lent had passed, he told the poor boy on the following Sunday to visit him, and when he entered told him to put his tongue out from his mouth and show it to him. Taking him by the chin, he pressed on his tongue with the sign of the holy cross, and after doing so told him to take back his tongue into his mouth and speak.

'In his monastery of In Derawuda, meaning the wood of the Deiri'

Beverley Minster.

'He was invited to dedicate the church of a nobleman ...'

The Saxon church at Escomb in County Durham, dating from the mid-seventh century, is a likely example of the private chapels of noblemen to which Bede refers in his chapters on John of Beverley.

'Say a word,' he said; 'say *gae*,' this being the English word of affirmation and agreement, meaning yes. His tongue was loosed, and he at once said what he had been told. The bishop added the names of the letters. 'Say A.' He said A. 'Say B.' He said this too. When he had repeated the names of the letters one at a time, the bishop went on to speak syllables and words for him to pronounce. And when he had repeated them all, he taught him to speak longer sentences, and he did so; and according to those who were present, for the whole of that day and the following night, as long as he could stay awake, he never ceased to speak and to reveal to others his secret thoughts and wishes, which he had never been able to do before. He was like that man who had long been lame and was healed by the apostles Peter and John, and stood up, leapt and walked; and went in with them to the Temple, walking and leaping and praising the Lord, rejoicing to have the use of his legs, of which he had been deprived for so long.

The bishop shared his joy at his recovery and ordered a doctor to attend also to curing the scabs on his head. The doctor did as he was bidden, and with the help of the bishop's blessing and prayers his skin was healed and he grew a beautiful head of hair; and he became a young man of clear complexion, ready speech and beautiful curly hair, having previously been disfigured, poor and dumb. And so, delighted to find himself healed, he chose to return home, though the bishop also invited him to live in his household.

✛

HE HEALS A SICK GIRL BY PRAYER

Ecclesiastical History of the English People Book V Chapter 3

Berthun also related another miracle performed by Bishop John. After Wilfrid, that most reverend man, was recalled as bishop of the church of Hagustaldesea after a long exile, and John himself succeeded to the bishopric of Eboracum on the death of Bosa, a man of great saintliness and humility, John once visited a nunnery at a place called Wetadun, over which Abbess Hereburg then presided.

'When we came there,' Berthun said, 'and had been welcomed by them all with great rejoicing, the abbess told us that one of the nuns, who was her own daughter, was afflicted with a grievous illness. Her arm had recently been bled, and while she was under treatment she was gripped by a sudden pain which quickly increased, so that her wounded arm grew worse and became so swollen that it could scarcely be encircled with both hands. She lay on her bed in such great pain that she seemed about to die. The abbess therefore asked the bishop if he would consent to go in to her and bless her, as she believed that she would soon get better if he blessed or touched her.

'He asked her when the girl had been bled, and learning that it was on the fourth day of the moon, said: "It was very unwise and ignorant of you to bleed her on the fourth day of the moon. I remember that Archbishop Theodore of blessed memory said that it was very dangerous to bleed at the time of the waxing of the moon and the rising of the Ocean tide. And what can I do for the girl, if she is going to die?"

'But the abbess implored him more urgently on behalf of her daughter, whom she loved greatly and had planned to make abbess in her place. At last she persuaded him to go in to the sick girl. So, taking me with him, he went in to the maiden who was lying, as I have said, in the grip of severe pain and with her arm so swollen that she could not bend her elbow at all. Standing by her he said a prayer over her, blessed her and went out.

'Later, while we were sitting at dinner at the usual hour, someone came and called me outside. He said, using the girl's name: "Cwenburg begs you to return to her quickly." I did so, and when I went in I found her looking more cheerful and apparently in good health. And when I sat with her she said: "Shall we get something to drink?"

'"Yes," I said, "and I shall be delighted if you can drink." A cup was brought, and we both drank, and she told me what had happened: "As soon as the bishop went out after praying for me and blessing me, I at once began to get better; even though I have not yet recovered my former strength, all the pain has completely disappeared, both from my arm, where it was more severe, and from my whole body, just as if the bishop took it outside with him. However, my arm still remains swollen, it seems."

'But when we left there, the dreadful swelling disappeared from her arm at once, just as the pain had disappeared from her limbs; and the maiden, rescued from death and suffering, gave praise to the Lord her Saviour together with His other servants who were there.'

✝

HE HEALS THE SICK WIFE OF A NOBLEMAN WITH HOLY WATER

Ecclesiastical
History of the
English People
Book V
Chapter 4

Abbot Berthun told the story of another similar miracle performed by Bishop John, as follows:

'Not far, less than two miles in fact, from our monastery, was the estate of a nobleman called Puch, whose wife had been suffering for about forty days from a most acute illness, so that for three weeks it had not been possible to carry her out of the bedroom in which she was lying. Now at that time the man of God happened to be invited there by the nobleman to dedicate a church, and after the dedication he was invited into his house for dinner. The bishop declined, saying that he ought to return to the monastery, which was close by. But the nobleman pressed his request more insistently, and vowed to give alms to the poor if only the bishop would agree to enter his house that day to break his fast. I too joined in his request, promising also to give alms to support the needy if he would enter the nobleman's house to dine and give a blessing.

'At length and with difficulty we obtained our request, and we went in to dinner. The bishop had sent one of the brothers who had come with me to take to the woman lying ill some of the holy water which he had blessed for the dedication of the church, instructing him to give it her to drink and to wash her with the water where he found her to be in most pain. When this was done, the woman at once arose fully cured, and feeling free of her long sickness and also restored to her long-lost strength, she brought the cup to the bishop and us and continued to serve us with drink till dinner was finished. In so doing she imitated the mother-in-law of blessed Peter, who after being sick of a fever arose at the touch of the Lord's hand, her health and strength restored, and ministered to them.'

✝

HE RECALLS A NOBLEMAN'S SERVANT FROM DEATH BY HIS PRAYERS

On another occasion he was invited to dedicate the church of a nobleman named Addi, and after performing the service requested of him he was asked by the nobleman to visit a young manservant of his who had lost all the use of his limbs, and was so seriously ill that he seemed on the point of death. Indeed, a coffin had already been prepared for the burial of his body. The man wept, and urgently implored the bishop to go in and pray for him. The servant's life, he said, was of great personal concern to him, and he trusted that, if the bishop would be willing to lay his hand on him and bless him, he would get better at once.

Ecclesiastical History of the English People Book V Chapter 5

So the bishop went in there, and found everyone in tears and the servant now very close to death, with the coffin in which he was to be laid for burial set by his side. He said a prayer and blessed him, and as he left spoke the usual words of comfort, 'I wish you a swift recovery.' Later, while they were sitting at table, the servant sent to his master asking him to send him a cup of wine, as he was thirsty. His master was overjoyed that he could drink, and sent him a goblet of wine blessed by the bishop. He drank it, got up at once, shook off his sickness and languor, and dressed himself. He then left his room, and went in and greeted the bishop and the other guests, saying that he would love to eat and drink with them himself. Overjoyed at his recovery, they told him to sit with them at dinner, and he sat and ate and drank and made merry just like one of the guests. He lived for many years afterwards, continuing to enjoy the good health that had been given him.

The story of this miracle was told by the abbot, who states that he was not present when it happened, but it was reported to him by the people who were there.

✠

BY HIS PRAYERS AND BLESSINGS HE SAVES FROM DEATH
ONE OF HIS CLERICS WHO HAS BEEN HURT BY A FALL

*Ecclesiastical
History of the
English People*
Book V
Chapter 6

I must not omit to mention the miracle which Christ's servant Herebald tells that the bishop performed on him. Herebald was then one of his clergy, but now rules as abbot over a monastery near the mouth of the river Tyne.

'As far as a man may judge,' he said, 'I found his way of life, which as a member of his household I knew very well, to be in all respects worthy of a bishop. But as to his worth in the judgement of Him who sees into men's hearts, this I have discovered through the experience of many others and through my own experience especially, in that he rescued me, so to say, from the very threshold of death and brought me back to the path of life by his prayers and blessing.

'In my early youth I lived among his clergy, occupied in the study of reading and singing, but my spirit was not yet fully trained to forsake youthful pleasures. One day we were on a journey with him when we came upon a flat, open road, suitable for galloping our horses; and the young men who were with him, mostly laymen, began to ask the bishop to let them try out their horses against each other at the gallop. He at first refused, saying that their request was frivolous; but at last he gave way to the unanimous wish of them all, saying, "Do so if you wish, but on condition that Herebald takes no part in your race." At that I begged him earnestly that I too might have a chance to race with them, as I had faith in my fine horse, which the bishop himself had given me; but I was quite unable to persuade him.

'They galloped their horses repeatedly back and forth while the bishop and I watched, and, unable to restrain myself, I gave way to temptation in spite of his command, and joined them in their sport and began to race with them. As I did so, I heard him behind me say with a sigh, "Oh, what distress you cause me by riding like this!" Although I heard, yet I persisted in the forbidden sport; and in no time, as my fiery horse took a great leap across a hollow in the road, I slid off and fell to the ground, and lay unconscious and quite still as if dead. For at that spot there was a stone level with the ground and covered by a thin layer of turf, although no other stone was to be found anywhere in the whole of the plain; and it chanced, or rather divine providence brought it about to punish my disobedience, that I hit this stone with my head and the hand which I had put under my head as I fell, breaking my thumb and fracturing my skull. As I said, I lay just like a dead man; and as I could not be moved they put up a tent for me to lie in. It was about the seventh hour of the day, and from then until evening I remained still and as if dead; but I then revived a little and was carried home by my companions. I lay speechless the whole night, vomiting blood, as I had suffered internal injuries from my fall. The bishop was grief-stricken over my disastrous fall, as he was specially fond of me; and he refused to sleep that night with his clergy as usual, but stayed awake the whole night in solitary prayer, beseeching God in His mercy to save me, I suppose. Early in the morning he came in to me, said a prayer over me, and called me by my name; and when I awoke as if from a deep sleep, he asked me if I knew who it was who was speaking to me. Opening my eyes, I said: "Yes; you are my beloved bishop." "Can you live?" he said. "I can," I said, "by your prayers, if it is the Lord's will."

'Placing his hand on my head and speaking a blessing, he returned to his prayers. A little later he came to me again and found me sitting up and now able to speak; and urged by divine prompting, as soon became apparent, he began to ask me if I knew beyond any doubt that I had been baptized. I replied that I was quite sure that I had been washed in the water of salvation for the remission of sins, and I told him the name of the priest by whom I knew I had been baptized. But he said: "If you were baptized by this priest, you are not fully baptized. I know him, and I know that when he was ordained priest he was so slow-witted that he was quite incapable of learning the office of catechism or baptism. For this reason I ordered him not to presume to exercise this ministry, because he could not perform it properly." With these words he set about catechizing me there and then, and his breathing into my face at once made me feel better. He called a doctor and ordered him to set and bind up my fractured skull. After receiving his blessing I soon became so much better that on the next day I mounted my horse and journeyed elsewhere with him; and before long I was fully cured and was washed in the water of life.'

He remained bishop for thirty-three years and then entered the Kingdom of Heaven, being buried in the chapel of St Peter, in his monastery of In Derawuda, in the year of our Lord 721. When his advancing years prevented him from administering his bishopric, he consecrated his priest Wilfrid to the see of Eboracum and retired to his monastery, where he ended his life in a manner pleasing to God.

Wilfrid of Hexham

No churchman portrayed by Bede was so clearly a forerunner of the powerful prince bishops of later medieval times as Wilfrid of Hexham.

Born of a noble family, Wilfrid was no hermit priest and, although he first experienced monastic life on Aidan's Lindisfarne, he had nothing in common with the ancient Celtic tradition. He was an ecclesiastical aristocrat dealing in power and land and moving as easily among the pinnacles of power in papal Rome as at the courts of English kings. He was the missionary who achieved the conversion of the South Saxons, the forceful theologian who carried the day at the Council of Whitby, and the great builder in stone who raised again Paulinus' church at York.

Wilfrid was, above all, a prince of the Church whose destiny hung on the rise and fall of kings. When he left home — in retreat from an unkind stepmother, according to tradition — he made his way to the court of Oswy where he soon became a protégé of Queen Eanfled. At eighteen he was already looking towards Rome, and Eanfled's Kentish connections speeded his journey to the continent. On his return to Northumbria he won the patronage of Alchfrith, sub-king of Deira under his father Oswy. By 664, the thirty-year-old Wilfrid had founded his great church at Ripon — Bede's In Hrypum — and won the great debate at Whitby. He travelled again to the continent and returned from Gaul to find his patron Alchfrith had suffered death in rebellion against Oswy. Yet Wilfrid's star continued to rise, reaching its zenith when Oswy was succeeded by Egfrith, whose queen Etheldreda held Wilfrid in the highest regard. It was certainly Etheldreda's influence that secured the land for Wilfrid's great foundation at Hexham.

When Etheldreda abandoned her husband's court for the religious life, Wilfrid's fortunes began to falter. His close association with the virgin queen did not endear him to Egfrith the warrior king, who saw him now as a powerful rival rather than a father confessor. Their inevitable quarrel cost Wilfrid his great estates and drove him back to Rome in search of papal allies. Wilfrid returned with letters of mandate from influential bishops and even from Pope Agatho himself, but Egfrith's response was to throw him into prison. After nine months of harsh imprisonment Wilfrid was released into exile, returning to Northumbria only when Aldfrith became king on the death of Egfrith. There was an uneasy relationship between the Irish-educated Aldfrith and the Roman-inclined Wilfrid who was never again restored to the power he had enjoyed under Etheldreda's patronage.

Wilfrid went once more to the continent, but his health was already failing. When the child-king Osred succeeded Aldfrith, Wilfrid — now over seventy — returned again to Northumbria to plead his case in synod on the river Nidd in 705 and to spend his last years at Ripon and Hexham on the estates secured for him by papal edict.

There are two major contemporary sources for our knowledge of Wilfrid of Hexham. Bede's *Historia* is one, but by far the fullest is the *Life* written by Eddius Stephanus, a monk of Ripon, within a decade of Wilfrid's death. Eddius wrote his account some ten years before Bede completed his own history and it must have been Bede's principal manuscript source on Wilfrid, especially as Eddius' *Life* was commissioned by Acca, Wilfrid's successor at Hexham and a good friend of Bede. We know from Bede's chapter on Etheldreda of Ely that he was personally acquainted with Wilfrid and he would certainly have spoken with people who had known Wilfrid well for many years. Indeed, Bede's own first abbot, Benedict Biscop, met the young Wilfrid at the Kentish court and set out with him on his first journey to Rome.

But for all his wealth of first-hand sources, Bede's chapters on Wilfrid still seem to lack the sympathy he showed for other prominent figures such as Aidan, Cuthbert and even John of Beverley. D.H. Farmer — translator of Eddius and an authority on Wilfrid — suggests that Bede's 'long notice of Wilfrid, although factual and accurate, lacks warmth, resembling in spirit an obituary in The Times.' This seems all the more strange because Wilfrid's fervent commitment to all things Roman should have greatly inspired the apparently like-minded Bede. Perhaps Wilfrid's passion for power and land rather than books and learning was alien to the scholar monk and whatever Bede's formal regard for the Roman orthodoxy, he retained his warmth for the fathers of the old Celtic tradition whom Wilfrid had so decisively vanquished.

Looking back over the centuries, the modern reader might be forgiven for the suspicion that, however impressive his achievements, Wilfrid of Hexham was perhaps not remembered by Bede as the most likeable of men.

✛

CENRED, KING OF THE MERCIANS, AND OFFA, KING OF THE EAST SAXONS,
END THEIR LIFE IN ROME IN THE MONASTIC HABIT.
THE LIFE AND DEATH OF BISHOP WILFRID

In the fourth year of Osred's reign, Cenred, who for some time *Ecclesiastical* had reigned most honourably over the Mercians, relinquished *History of the* the kingship still more honourably. He came to Rome, where he *English People* received the tonsure and became a monk during the pontificate Book V of Constantine, and he remained there till the day of his death, Chapter 19 devoting himself to prayer, fasting and almsgiving at the shrines of the apostles. Ceolred, son of Cenred's predecessor Aethelred, succeeded to the throne in his place. Cenred was accompanied to Rome by the son of Sighere, king of the East Saxons; he was a handsome and lovable young man named Offa, and it was the fervent wish of all his people that he would occupy and retain the kingship. With the same devout purpose as Cenred, he left his wife, his lands, his kinsmen and his native land for the sake of Christ and for the sake of the Gospel; in order that he might receive a hundredfold in this life, and in the world to come, life everlasting. He too, therefore, when they came to the holy places of Rome, was tonsured and finished his life in the monastic habit, and then attained to that vision of the blessed apostles in Heaven that he had long desired.

In the same year that they left Britain, the renowned Bishop Wilfrid died in the district of In Undalum, after being bishop for forty-five years; and his body was placed in a coffin and carried to his monastery at In Hrypum, where it was buried in the church of the blessed apostle Peter with the honour due to so great a prelate. Let us now go back and recall briefly the events of his life. He was a boy of good character and virtuous beyond his years, so disciplined and prudent in all his behaviour that his elders deservedly loved and respected him and took him to their hearts as one of themselves. At the age of fourteen he chose the monastic in preference to the secular life. His mother was already dead, and when he told his father of his decision he gladly supported the boy's spiritual longings and aspirations

and told him to persevere in the way of salvation which he had
chosen. So he came to the island of Lindisfarne and offered
himself for the service of the monks, taking every care to learn
and practise the monastic life of chastity and devotion. Having a
quick understanding, he very soon learned the psalms and some
other books, and although he was not yet tonsured he was
conspicuous for those virtues of humility and obedience which
are more important than the tonsure. For this reason he was
held in deserved affection both by the older monks and by his
peers. After serving God in this monastery for some years, the
shrewd young man gradually realized that the path of virtuous
life laid down by the Irish was by no means perfect, and he
determined to go to Rome and see what ecclesiastical and monastic practices were observed in the Apostolic See. When he
told the brothers of his decision, they approved of it and urged
him to carry out his plan. He came at once to Queen Eanfled,
because he was known to her and it was through her advice and
request that he had joined the monastery. He told her of his
desire to visit the shrines of the blessed apostles, and, delighted
at the youth's honourable resolve, she sent him to King Earconbert of Kent, her uncle's son, asking him that Wilfrid might be
respectfully conveyed to Rome. The archbishop there at that
time was Honorius, one of the disciples of the blessed Pope
Gregory, and a man deeply versed in ecclesiastical affairs. The
quick-minded young man stayed there for some time devoting
himself to learning everything he saw, until another arrived
there named Benedict Biscop, an English nobleman who also
wished to go to Rome.

The king, therefore, gave Wilfrid to Biscop for a companion,
with orders to take him with him to Rome. When they reached
Lugdunum, Wilfrid was detained there by Dalfinus, bishop of
the city, while Benedict pressed on with the journey and reached
Rome. The bishop was delighted by the young man's wise conversation, by the grace and beauty of his countenance, by his
promptness in action, and by the steadiness and maturity of his
mind. So he gave Wilfrid and his companions, as long as they
stayed with him, a generous supply of all they needed; and
furthermore, he offered to put him in charge, if he wished, of a

St Wilfrid's Chair, Hexham Abbey.

A bishop's seat — or *cathedra* — carved from a single block of stone and
dating from AD 681.

large part of Gaul, to give him his brother's unmarried daughter for his wife, and to adopt him as his son. Wilfrid thanked him for the kindness that he had thought fit to show him, though a stranger, but answered that he had resolved upon another way of life and that it was for this reason that he had left his native land and begun the journey to Rome.

Hearing this, the bishop sent him to Rome, giving him a guide and a plentiful supply of everything that he needed for the journey; and he requested most insistently that when he returned to his native land he should remember to visit him on the way. When Wilfrid came to Rome, he applied himself daily to prayer and the study of ecclesiastical subjects, as he had intended, and he made the friendship of a most holy and learned man, Archdeacon Boniface, who was also a counsellor to the Pope. Through his teaching he studied the four gospels one after another, and from the same teacher he learned the correct method of calculating Easter and many other matters of Church discipline which he had no means of learning in his native land. After spending some months there in successful study, he returned to Dalfinus in Gaul, staying with him for three years and receiving the tonsure from him. The bishop was so fond of him that he intended to make him his successor, but this was prevented when he was cut off by a cruel death, and Wilfrid was saved for a bishopric among his own people, the English. Queen Baldhild had sent soldiers and ordered the bishop to be put to death, and Wilfrid, being one of his clergy, followed him to the place where he was to be beheaded, wishing to die with him, in spite of the bishop's protestations. But when the executioners learned that he was a foreigner and of English birth, they spared him and refused to kill him with their bishop.

Wilfrid came to Britain and became a friend of King Alchfrith, who had learned always to follow and cherish the Catholic rules of the Church. When he found that Wilfrid was Catholic, he at once gave him ten hides of land at a place called Stanford, and not long afterwards a monastery with thirty hides at a place named In Hrypum. He had previously given this land for the founding of a monastery to the followers of the Irish, but later, when offered the choice, they chose to leave the place rather than accept the Catholic Easter and the other canonical rites practised by the Roman and Apostolic Church; so he gave it to Wilfrid, seeing him to be trained in better rules and observances.

At this time, and at the King's bidding, he was ordained priest in this monastery by Agilbert, bishop of the Gewissas, mentioned above, because the king desired that a man of such learning and devotion should be a priest and teacher specially favoured by being in constant attendance on him. Not long after, when the Irish sect, as explained already, had been exposed and banished, the king sent Wilfrid to Gaul, on the advice and with the consent of his father Oswy, asking that he might be consecrated as his bishop by that same Agilbert who was now acting as bishop of Paris. Wilfrid was about thirty years old. Eleven other bishops joined Agilbert for the consecration, and performed the service with great dignity. While Wilfrid remained overseas, a holy man named Chad was consecrated to the see of Eboracum on King Oswy's order, as related above. He ruled the church with distinction for three years, and then retired to look after his monastery at Laestingaei, while Wilfrid took over the bishopric of the whole kingdom of Northumbria.

He was later expelled from the see during the reign of Egfrith, and other bishops were consecrated in his place, as described above. He intended to go to Rome and plead his cause before the Pope, but after embarking on his ship he was driven by the west wind to Frisia. Here he was given an honourable reception by the barbarians and their king Aldgisl, and preached Christ to them, giving many thousands of them instruction in the word of truth and washing away the filth of their sins in the Saviour's font. He was the first to undertake there that work of the Gospel which was later completed with great devotion by Christ's most reverend bishop Wilbrord. He spent the winter there happily with God's new people, and then resumed his journey to Rome; and when his case was discussed in the presence of Pope Agatho and many bishops, it was decided by their unanimous judgement that he had been wrongly accused and that he was worthy of the bishopric.

At that time Pope Agatho summoned to Rome a synod of a hundred and twenty-five bishops, in opposition to those who

taught that there was only one will and operation in our Lord
and Saviour. He ordered Wilfrid, too, to be called and to sit
among the bishops and declare his own faith and that of the
kingdom and island from which he had come. When it was
found that Wilfrid and his people were of Catholic faith, it was
decided to include this among the other acts of the synod, and it
was recorded in the following words: 'Wilfrid, beloved of God,
bishop of the city of Eboracum, appealing concerning his case to
the Apostolic See and being acquitted by its authority of all
charges, both specified and unspecified; and with a hundred and
twenty-five other bishops being appointed to sit in judgement in
the synod; did confess the true and Catholic faith, on behalf of
all the northern part of Britain and Ireland, and the islands
inhabited by the English, the British, the Irish and the Picts; and
did confirm it with his signature.'

After this he returned to Britain and converted the kingdom
of the South Saxons from idolatrous worship to the faith of
Christ. He also sent ministers of the Word to the Isle of Wight;
and in the second year of Aldfrith, Egfrith's successor, he was
restored to his episcopal see at the king's invitation. But five
years later he was again accused, and was driven from the
bishopric by that same king and several bishops; whereupon he
went to Rome, and was given an opportunity to defend himself,
in the presence of his accusers, before Pope John and many
bishops. By their unanimous judgement it was decided that his
accusers had in part devised false charges against him, and the
Pope wrote to the English kings Aethelred and Aldfrith, request-
ing them to restore him to his bishopric, as he had been unjustly
condemned.

His acquittal was assisted by the reading of the acts of the
synod of Pope Agatho of blessed memory, which had been held,
as described above, when Wilfrid was present in the city of
Rome and sitting in council among the bishops. When, as the
case required, the acts of this synod were read for several days,
on the Pope's order, before the nobility and a large crowd of
people, they came to the place where these words were written:
'Wilfrid, beloved of God, bishop of the city of Eboracum, appealing concerning his case to the Apostolic See and being acquitted

The Anglo-Saxon Crypt, Hexham Abbey.

Wilfrid's masons brought the stone for his abbey at Hexham from nearby Roman *Corstopitum*, modern Corbridge in Northumberland. The criss-cross carving and fragments of Roman inscription can still be clearly seen in the crypt at Hexham which survives from Wilfrid's foundation of the abbey.

by its authority of all charges, both specified and unspecified,'
and so on, as quoted above. When this was read, they heard it
with astonishment, and when the reader fell silent began to ask
each other who this Bishop Wilfrid was. Then Boniface, the
Pope's counsellor, and many others who had seen him there in
the time of Pope Agatho, said that he was the bishop who had
been accused by his countrymen and had recently come to Rome
to be judged by the Apostolic See. 'He came here long ago,' they
said, 'on a similar charge. The case and the dispute between the
two parties was quickly heard, and judgement given by Pope
Agatho of blessed memory, who decided that he had been
unlawfully driven from his bishopric. The Pope held him in such
great esteem that he ordered him to sit in the council of bishops
that he had summoned, as a man of incorrupt faith and honest
mind.' When they heard this, it was the verdict of them all,
including the Pope himself, that a man of such authority, who
had held office as bishop for nearly forty years, ought not to be
condemned, but should return to his country with honour, fully
acquitted of the charges made against him.

On his arrival in Gaul when returning to Britain, he suddenly
became ill, and his condition worsened so that he was unable to
ride his horse and was carried by his servants in a litter. He was
brought like this to the city of Maeldum in Gaul, and lay for
four days and nights as if dead, his faint breathing being the
only evidence that he was alive. He continued so for four days
and nights without food or drink, speechless and hearing nothing, but at last, on the fifth day he arose and sat up, as if
roused from a deep sleep. Opening his eyes he saw round him a
company of brothers chanting psalms as they wept, and with a
little sigh he asked where the priest Acca was. The priest was
called at once, and when he came in and saw that he was better
and now able to speak, he knelt and gave thanks to God with
all the brothers who were there. After they had sat for a little
time talking anxiously about the judgements of Heaven, the
bishop ordered the others to go out for a while and addressed
the priest Acca as follows: 'A fearful vision appeared to me just
now, which I wish you to hear and keep secret until I know
what God wishes to become of me. There stood by me someone

resplendent in white robes, saying that he was Michael the Archangel, and he said: "I have been sent to recall you from death; for the Lord has granted you life through the prayers and tears of your disciples and brothers, and through the intercession of His blessed mother, Mary ever virgin. Therefore I tell you, that for the present you will be cured of this illness; but be prepared, for after four years I shall return to visit you. You will reach your native land and recover most of the possessions which were taken from you, and you will end your life in peace and tranquillity.'" So the bishop recovered, and all rejoiced and gave thanks to God. He then set out and arrived in Britain.

When they read the letters which he had brought from the Pope, Archbishop Bertwald and Aethelred, formerly king but now an abbot, supported his cause very readily; and Aethelred sent for Cenred, whom he had made king in his place, asking him to befriend the bishop, and he agreed. Aldfrith, however, king of the Northumbrians, scorned to make him welcome; but he did not survive long, and so it came about that early in the reign of his son Osred a synod was held at the river Nidd, and after some argument on both sides he was finally restored to the bishopric of his church by their unanimous agreement. And so for four years, until the day of his death, he lived in peace. He died in his monastery in the district of Undalum, while Abbot Cuthbald was in charge of it; and he was carried by the brothers to his first monastery at In Hrypum, and buried in the church of the blessed apostle Peter, next to the altar on the south side, as mentioned above. His epitaph was inscribed over him as follows:

> Wilfrid lies buried here, who by devout intent
> Possessed, great bishop, to the Lord did build this
>   church;
> And dedicated it in glorious Peter's name,
> To whom the keys of Heaven by Christ, earth's Judge,
>   were given;
> And lovingly in gold and Tyrian purple clothed it.

Herein on high he raised the trophy of the Cross
In gleaming gold; commanded, too, the Gospels four
In order to be writ in lettering of gold,
Which in a worthy case of russet gold he placed.
He to the solemn Paschal feast its season due,
Fixed by our Fathers and by Catholic doctrine taught,
Restored; all error and confusion swept away,
He showed his people sure observance for their guide.
Within these walls a goodly company of monks
He gathered, and with care instructed in the Rule
Established by the Fathers; tossed about long years
By many trials at home and many overseas,
Thrice fifteen years a bishop's duties he fulfilled,
Then passed to rest, and sought with joy the realms of
        Heaven.
Grant, Jesus, that his flock their shepherd's path may tread.

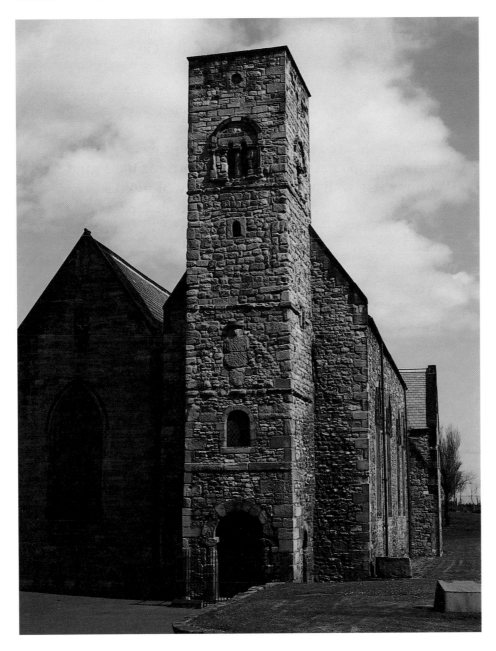

'A monastery in honour of Peter, the most blessed chief of the apostles, at the mouth of the river Wear on its north bank'

The largely original west front of St Peter's Church, Monkwearmouth.

From the
Lives of the Abbots of Wearmouth and Jarrow

The *Historia Abbatum* — Bede's *Lives of the Abbots of Wearmouth and Jarrow* — is a document of great importance, a factual first-hand account of Saxon monastic life written by the outstanding historian of the early Middle Ages.

Writing of events to which he himself was witness, Bede tells of five abbots: Benedict Biscop who first established the dual foundation, Ceolfrith the first abbot of St Paul's at Jarrow, Eosterwin who took charge of Wearmouth when Biscop set out on his last journey to Rome, Sigurd who succeeded Eosterwin, and Hwaetbert who succeeded Ceolfrith at Jarrow.

The dual foundation of Wearmouth and Jarrow — 'Wiuraemuda and In Gyrwum' — was one of the great centres of civilization in eighth-century Christendom, renowned as a place of learning as well as for its celebrated historian-in-residence. The monastery, like Bede himself, drew enormous benefit from the whole spectrum of monastic and cultural traditions of its time. Links with the Irish Church are confirmed by the two visits to Jarrow of Adamnan, abbot of Iona, in 686 and 688, while in 710, Nechtan, king of the Picts, sent to Ceolfrith for guidance on monastic practice. Benedict Biscop's continental travels established links with Rome and Gaul, as well as the old Roman centres in Provence. Wearmouth/Jarrow — almost alone among the monasteries of Northumbria — was much enriched by its two-way exchange of Irish, Pictish and Roman monastic traditions.

The importance of Wearmouth/Jarrow is reflected in the importance of Bede's *Historia Abbatum* which was certainly written sometime after Ceolfrith's death in 716, and probably earlier than the anonymous *Life of Ceolfrith*.

From the *Historia Abbatum* I have selected chapters on the two abbots most closely connected with Bede himself.

Benedict Biscop was the man into whose care Bede's parents commended their seven-year-old son in the year 680. He was born to a Northumbrian noble family, possibly of Romano-British origin, in 628 and his family name — according to Eddius — was Baducing. He probably adopted the name of Benedict when he took holy orders, while Biscop was effectively an ecclesiastical title.

He abandoned a military career at the age of twenty-five to pursue his cultural and monastic interests. At the Kentish court he met the young Wilfrid and set out with him for Rome. When Wilfrid paused in Gaul, Biscop pressed on to arrive in Rome in the year 654. He was certainly the first Northumbrian, and probably the first Englishman, to visit Rome since the end of the *Pax Romana*. Between 654 and 665 he is said to have visited seventeen monasteries in Italy and Gaul. From 665 to 667, we find him at the island monastery of Lérins off the southern coast of France, where he finally took the tonsure. In 667 he was again in Rome before returning to England in the company of Theodore, the learned Greek newly appointed as archbishop of Canterbury. Biscop served as abbot at Canterbury before journeying home to Northumbria, where he was granted lands by King Egfrith on which to found his monastery at Wearmouth.

Benedict Biscop was a tireless traveller who made at least five journeys to Rome. On his continental travels he collected the books and treasures for Wearmouth and the craftsmen, skilled in stone and glass working, to build and decorate his monastery 'in the Roman manner.'

Bede's portrait of him describes a man of learning and civilized taste, a lover of books and patron of the arts. His monastery, with its magnificent library and accompanying scriptorium, was one of the great achievements of Northumbria's golden age, but his enduring legacy remains the work of Bede himself, because it is no exaggeration to suggest that without Benedict Biscop there would have been no Venerable Bede.

Ceolfrith, the monk of Wearmouth appointed by Biscop as the first abbot of Jarrow, was Bede's mentor during the formative years when Biscop was so often travelling abroad.

Ceolfrith saw his task as the continuation of the work that Biscop had begun at Wearmouth/Jarrow. He shared Biscop's passion for books and greatly enlarged the monastic library. The scriptorium flourished under Ceolfrith, producing the three great bibles — or 'pandects' as they were known — that stood as the masterpieces of the calligraphic art of Wearmouth and Jarrow. Their text was drawn from the *Codex Grandior* of Cassiodorus of Vivarium, a manuscript of St Jerome's translation brought back by Biscop and surely the subject of hours of study by Bede. The three pandects — one each for the altars of St Peter's at Wearmouth and St Paul's at Jarrow and one intended as Ceolfrith's gift to Rome — were written in the polished uncial script of Biscop's scriptorium.

Bede offers a moving account of the departure of Ceolfrith from Wearmouth, setting out at the age of seventy-four to retrace the journey

'He sent to Gaul to bring back glass-makers, craftsmen as yet unknown in Britain, to glaze the windows of the church'

The oldest coloured window glass in Europe — originally in the monastic refectory — is mounted in the seventh-century stone window of the chancel of St Paul's Church at Jarrow.

'A monastery dedicated to the blessed apostle Paul'

The seventh-century oratory of Bede's monastery survives today as the chancel of St Paul's Church, Jarrow.

to Rome that he had undertaken so many years before in company with Benedict Biscop. Ceolfrith did not reach the eternal city. He died *en route* at Langres in Gaul, but the great bible was carried on to Rome where it disappeared from view for over a thousand years.

Somehow Ceolfrith's pandect found its way to the monastery of Monte Amiata, ninety miles north of Rome, from where the *Codex Amiatinus* — now in the Laurentian Library, Florence — has been proved to be the same book with which Ceolfrith set out for Rome. Careful comparison of its dedication page with the text of Ceolfrith's original dedication recorded in the anonymous *Life* — supported by ultra-violet photography — confirms this splendid bible as the greatest surviving achievement of the scribes of Wearmouth and Jarrow.

The *Codex Amiatinus* remains today as the wholly characteristic legacy of Ceolfrith of Jarrow, the abbot whose delight in the books of the great library was rivalled only by his enthusiasm for his work in the monastic bakehouse.

✢

BENEDICT BISCOP

Lives of the Abbots of Wearmouth and Jarrow Chapter 1

Christ's devout servant Benedict Biscop, inspired by divine grace, built a monastery in honour of Peter, the most blessed chief of the apostles, at the mouth of the river Wear on its north bank. He received help and a grant of land from the venerable and holy Egfrith, the king of that people, and he ruled over the monastery for sixteen years with the same care and devotion as he had shown in building it, despite the burden of his frequent travels and periods of illness. To quote the words in which blessed Pope Gregory honours the life of an abbot of the same name: 'He was a man of venerable life, rightly named Benedict because blessed by God's grace; from his boyhood he had an old man's heart and a moral character beyond his years, never surrendering to sensual pleasure.' He was of English race and noble birth, but with an equal nobility of mind he was always intent on winning a place among the company of the angels. For example, when he was twenty-five and a thane of King Oswy he received from the king a grant of land befitting his rank, but he disdained the possession that perishes that he might gain that which is eternal; he despised earthly warfare with its corruptible reward, that he might fight for the true King and prove worthy of an eternal crown in the City of Heaven; he left his home, his family and his country for the sake of Christ and the Gospel, that he might receive a hundredfold and gain eternal life; he scorned the bondage of carnal marriage that he might follow the Lamb of spotless virginity in the Kingdom of Heaven; and he abstained from the procreation of mortal children of the flesh, being predestined by Christ to bring up sons for Him by spiritual instruction who would live for ever in the life of Heaven.

✛

He therefore left his native land and went to Rome, where he took care to visit in person and venerate the tombs of the blessed apostles, in fulfilment of a long and ardent desire; and on returning home he continued with all his heart to love and honour and make known to anyone he could the practices he had observed in the life of that Church. At that time Alchfrith, King Oswy's son, also arranged to go to Rome to venerate the shrines of the apostles, and invited Benedict to accompany him on the journey. Alchfrith was forbidden by his father to carry out his intended journey and ordered to remain at home in his own kingdom, but Benedict, being a young man of good character, quickly completed the journey he had undertaken and in great haste came again to Rome. It was during the time when Vitalian, of blessed memory, was Pope. As before, Benedict drank many sweet draughts of health-giving knowledge, and then after several months he left Rome for the island of Lérins, where he joined the company of the monks, received the tonsure, took monastic vows, and duly observed the discipline of the Rule with meticulous care. After being instructed for two years in the monastic way of life, he was again overcome by love of blessed Peter, the chief of the apostles, and decided to return to the city hallowed by his body.

Lives of the Abbots of Wearmouth and Jarrow Chapter 2

'Ceolfridus Anglorum ...'

The *Codex Amiatinus*. Of Ceolfrith's three great pandects, the
only one to survive intact is the bible with which he set out
for Rome on a June morning in the year 716. After his death
at Langres, some of his monks pressed on for Rome carrying
the pandect with them. At that point it disappeared from
view until it was rediscovered in the late nineteenth century
at the monastery of Monte Amiata where the manuscript
bible known as the *Codex Amiatinus* has been proved to be
that which Ceolfrith intended as his gift for Rome. The design shows the influence of Cassiodorus, whose *Codex Grandior* was in the library of Wearmouth/Jarrow, and the text
from the Vulgate of St Jerome — the 'new translation of the
scriptures' to which Bede refers — is written in formal
Roman uncials. The conclusive item of proof appears on the
dedication page shown here, where the text is identical with
the original dedication as recorded in the anonymous *Life of
Ceolfrith* — apart from the forged amendments clearly apparent in this photograph. The name *Petrus Langobardorum* —
'Peter of the Lombards' — has been inserted where the original *Ceolfridus Anglorum* — 'Ceolfrith of the English' — has
been erased. Ultra-violet photography has provided the final
proof that this awesome volume is without question the long-
lost masterpiece of the scriptorium of Bede's monastery.

Biblioteca Medicea-Laurenziana, Florence: MS Amiatinus I.c. 1v

+ CENOBIUM AD EXIMII MERITO

 UENERABILES AL UXTORIS

QUEM CAPUT ECCLESIAE

 DEDICAT ALTA FIDES

PETRUS LANGOBARDORUM

 EXTREMIS DEFINIB· ABBAS

DEUOTI AFFECTUS

 PIGNORA MITTO MEI

MEQUE MEOSQ·OPTANS

 TANTI INTER GAUDIA PATRIS

INCAELIS MEMOREM

 SEMPER HABERE LOCUM

✢

Before long, with the arrival of a merchant ship, he had his wish. Now at that time Egbert, king of Kent, had sent from Britain a man named Wighard, who had been elected to the office of bishop and had been thoroughly instructed in all ecclesiastical usage by blessed Pope Gregory's Roman disciples in Kent. The king wanted him to be consecrated bishop in Rome in order to have a bishop of his own race and language, as he believed that he and the peoples subject to him would be more fully immersed in the Word and mysteries of the faith if they received them, not through an interpreter, but from the lips and the hand of a man who was their kinsman and of their own race. When Wighard reached Rome, he and all his companions on the journey caught the plague and died, and he was never consecrated bishop; but so that the death of the delegates might not rob a devout embassy of the faithful of its proper reward, the Pope took counsel and chose one of his own company to send to Britain as archbishop. He chose Theodore, a man learned in both secular and ecclesiastical knowledge and in both the Greek and the Latin languages; and as his colleague and counsellor he gave him Abbot Hadrian, a man of great energy and great prudence to match. And because he saw in the venerable Benedict the promise of a wise, industrious, devout and honourable man, he gave him charge of the newly consecrated bishop and all his companions, instructing him to abandon the pilgrimage he had undertaken for Christ, and return to his country with a still nobler purpose: he was to take to the king the teacher of the truth that he had so eagerly sought, and act as both interpreter and guide to Theodore on his journey to Britain and while he taught there. Benedict did as he had ordered. They came to Kent, where they were most favourably received; and Theodore was enthroned as archbishop, while Benedict took charge of the monastery of the blessed apostle Peter, of which Hadrian later became abbot.

After ruling the monastery for two years, he set out on his third journey from Britain to Rome, completing it as successfully as before, and brought back a large number of books on every branch of sacred knowledge, some bought at a favourable price, others given him by friends. At Vienne on his return journey he collected some books he had bought and deposited with friends there. On entering Britain he decided he should visit Cenwalch, king of the West Saxons, whose friendship he had enjoyed and whose kindness had helped him more than once. But just then Cenwalch died unexpectedly and before his time, and at length Benedict turned again to his own people and the land of his birth and came to visit Egfrith, king of the country beyond the Humber. He described to him everything he had done since leaving his native land as a young man; he revealed his intense longing for the religious life; he explained what he had learned at Rome and elsewhere of ecclesiastical and monastic practice; he told him how many sacred books and what precious relics of the blessed apostles and the martyrs of Christ he had brought back; and Egfrith felt so well disposed to him that he at once gave him seventy hides of his own land and ordered him to build a monastery on it in honour of the first pastor of the Church. This monastery was built in the year of our Lord 674.

Lives of the Abbots of Wearmouth and Jarrow
Chapter 4

Only a year after the foundation of the monastery, Benedict crossed the sea to Gaul, where he looked for stonemasons to build him a church of stone in the Roman style that he had always loved; and he hired some and brought them back. He displayed so much enthusiasm in the work of building the church, out of love of blessed Peter to whom it was to be dedicated, that within the space of a single year from the laying of the foundations the roof was in place, and you might have seen the solemn rites of the Mass being celebrated inside. As the work neared completion, he sent representatives to Gaul to bring back glass-makers, craftsmen as yet unknown in Britain, to glaze

Lives of the Abbots of Wearmouth and Jarrow
Chapter 5

OVERLEAF

Durham Cathedral

the windows of the church, its side-chapels and upper storey. This was done, and they arrived; and as well as completing the work asked of them, they helped the English people from that time to understand and learn the art of glass-making, an art whose fine products include lamps for the living-quarters of the church and vessels of many other kinds. In addition, Benedict's devotion led him to buy and have transported from overseas all the sacred vessels and vestments needed for the service of the altar and the church, because he could not obtain them at home.

Lives of the Abbots of Wearmouth and Jarrow
Chapter 6

Tireless in providing for his church, he determined that the means to adorn and protect it that were unobtainable even in Gaul should be brought from Rome; and after ordering his monastery under the life of a Rule, he completed his fourth journey there, and returned with a wealth of spiritual treasures more varied than ever before. First, he brought back a great number of books of every kind. Secondly, he brought a plentiful supply of relics of the blessed apostles and martyrs of Christ, to the future benefit of many English churches. Thirdly, he introduced into his monastery an order of chanting and psalmody and liturgical practice that conformed to the Roman pattern. He had asked Pope Agatho for permission to bring to Britain John, the chief cantor of the church of the blessed apostle Peter and abbot of the monastery of St Martin, that his English monastery might have a teacher from Rome. The Pope consented, and when John arrived he passed on his knowledge of Church practices in Rome, not only by speaking about them to the monks, but also by leaving a substantial written account which is still kept in the monastery library as a record of his teaching. Fourthly, Benedict brought the valuable gift of a letter of privilege from the venerable Pope Agatho, given in accordance with the permission, consent, wish and encouragement of King Egfrith, which guaranteed to his monastery security and freedom from all external interference in perpetuity. Fifthly, he brought back to adorn the church he had built to the blessed apostle Peter paintings of sacred subjects: a picture of the blessed Mother of God, Mary ever virgin, and of the twelve apostles, with which to span the central nave of the church from wall to wall on a wooden entablature; scenes from the gospels, to adorn the south wall of the church; and the visions of the Apocalypse of St John to adorn the north wall. His intention was that all who entered the church, even those unable to read, might gaze wherever they looked upon the sight, ever dear, of Christ and His saints, if only in a picture; might reflect more attentively on the blessing of the Lord's incarnation; and by having before their eyes the fateful scene of the Last Judgement might remember to examine themselves more strictly.

✤

And so King Egfrith, deeply impressed by the venerable Benedict's virtue, industry and devotion, and seeing that the land he had granted him for building a monastery had borne good fruit, increased his gift by the additional grant of an estate of forty hides. A year later, with King Egfrith's approval, or rather, at his bidding, Benedict sent about seventeen monks there with the priest Ceolfrith as abbot, and built a monastery dedicated to the blessed apostle Paul, on the understanding that the two foundations should be united in the same spirit of peace and harmony, and that mutual friendship and goodwill should obtain between them for all time. To use a simile, just as the body cannot be separated from the head by which it breathes, and the head cannot forget the body which is necessary to its life, so no one was to make any attempt to disrupt the bond of brotherhood which would unite these monasteries dedicated to the two chief apostles. Ceolfrith, whom Benedict appointed abbot, gave him unstinting help in everything from the earliest days of the founding of the first monastery, and had gone with him to Rome, when a suitable opportunity occurred, to learn what was needed and for worship. At this time also, Benedict chose Eosterwin, a monk of St Peter's, to place in charge of that monastery as abbot, so that the burden of work which was too much for him on his own might be borne more easily with the help of a worthy and

Lives of the Abbots of Wearmouth and Jarrow Chapter 7

'Hac sunt in fossa Baedae venerabilis ossa'

Bede's tomb in the Galilee Chapel of Durham Cathedral.

much loved fellow-soldier. It must not be thought inappropriate for a single monastery to have had two abbots at the same time. It was made necessary by Benedict's frequent absences on the monastery's behalf, his many journeys overseas and the uncertainty about the time of his return. History tells us that the blessed apostle Peter appointed two assistant bishops at Rome to rule the Church in turn as necessity arose; and the great Abbot Benedict himself, as blessed Pope Gregory relates, thought fit to put twelve abbots in charge of his disciples, thereby strengthening rather than weakening their bond of love.

Ceolfrith was a man industrious in everything he did, quick-minded, energetic, mature in judgement, and intensely dedicated to the religious life. As I mentioned earlier, under the direction and with the help of Benedict he first spent seven years in founding, bringing to completion and ruling over the monastery of the blessed apostle Paul; and he then for twenty-eight years exercised enlightened rule over both monasteries, or to speak more accurately, over the one monastery of the blessed apostles Peter and Paul founded on two separate sites. All the splendid works of piety begun by his predecessor he set himself to complete with equal energy. During his long period of rule he found it necessary to provide for many of the monastery's needs. He built more oratories, and he enlarged the stock of vessels for the altar and church and that of every kind of vestment. He doubled the number of books in the library of each monastery, with an energy equal to Abbot Benedict's urgency in founding them. For example, he had three pandects of the new translation of the scriptures copied to add to the copy of the old translation which he had brought back from Rome; and on his return to Rome in old age he took one of these with him among his gifts, leaving the other pair to the two monasteries. Also, in exchange for the book of the cosmographers, a wonderful piece of workmanship which Benedict had bought in Rome, he acquired from King Aldfrith, who was very learned in the scriptures, eight hides of land near the river Fresca which he assigned to the monastery of

Lives of the Abbots of Wearmouth and Jarrow Chapter 15 Ceolfrith

the blessed apostle Paul. Benedict himself while he was alive had agreed the terms of this exchange with King Aldfrith, but died before he could complete it. Later, however, during the reign of Osred, Ceolfrith exchanged this land, together with an appropriate payment, for twenty hides of land at a place known to the local people as the village of Sambuce, as the land was closer to the monastery. He sent monks to Rome during the papacy of Sergius of blessed memory, and received from him a letter of privilege granting protection to his monastery, similar to the one given to Benedict by Pope Agatho. This was brought to Britain and produced at a synod, where it was confirmed by the signatures of the bishops who were present and the noble King Aldfrith. The previous letter of privilege also, as is well known, had been publicly confirmed in synod in the same way by the king and bishops of that time. It was during Ceolfrith's time as abbot that Witmer, an aged and devout servant of Christ, as learned in every branch of secular knowledge as in knowledge of the scriptures, entered the monastery of the blessed apostle Peter, which Ceolfrith ruled over, and gave ten hides of land granted him by King Aldfrith, at the village of Daltun, to belong to that monastery in perpetuity.

Lives of the Abbots of Wearmouth and Jarrow
Chapter 16

Ceolfrith had for long observed the discipline of the Rule which its father and provider, with the authority of tradition, laid down for his own benefit and that of his community. He had applied himself unceasingly to the daily task of prayer and chant, of which he achieved an unrivalled mastery. He had been remarkably forceful in restraining wayward brothers, and equally discreet in comforting the weak. He had practised an abstinence in food and drink and a poverty of dress unusual among those in authority. Now that he was well advanced in years, he realized that his great age prevented him from setting a proper standard of spiritual discipline for those in his charge, whether by his teaching or his life; and after a long period of private reflection he decided it would be best to instruct the brothers to choose a more suitable father from among themselves, in accor-

dance with the terms of their privilege and the Rule of the holy
Abbot Benedict. He himself resolved to return to the shrines of
the blessed apostles in Rome, where as a young man he had
been with Benedict, so that before he died he might spend some
time released from the cares of the world and enjoy the freedom
of peace and retirement; while the brothers would observe the
duties of the life of the Rule more strictly, under the influence of
a younger abbot and teacher.

Although at first they all objected, and pleaded with him repeatedly on their knees, weeping and sobbing, his wish was carried
out. So strong was his desire to set out that he hastened on his
way three days after revealing the secrets of his plan to the
brothers. He was afraid that he might die before he could reach
Rome, as in fact happened, and he wanted to prevent his journey being delayed by friends or men of rank, who all held him
in high regard. He also wished to avoid being given money by
anyone which he could not repay at the time, as it had always
been his custom, if anyone gave him a gift, to repay it at once or
after a suitable interval with equal generosity. So on Thursday
the fourth of June, after Mass had been sung early in the morning in the church of Mary, the blessed and ever virgin Mother of
God, and in the church of the apostle Peter, with those present
making their communion, he at once prepared to depart. They
all assembled in the church of St Peter, and he himself, after
kindling the incense and saying a prayer at the altar, gave the
kiss of peace to them all, standing on the steps and holding the
thurible. They went out from there with the sound of their
weeping audible through the litanies, and entered the oratory of
the blessed martyr Lawrence in the brothers' dormitory facing
them. Speaking his last farewell, he urged them to preserve
mutual love and to rebuke offenders, as the Gospel commands;
to all who might have offended, he granted the favour of his
forgiveness and goodwill; and if there were any whom he had
censured too harshly, he besought them all to pray for him and
be at peace with him. They came to the shore, and again, as they

*Lives of the
Abbots of
Wearmouth
and Jarrow*
Chapter 17

wept, he gave them all the kiss of peace. They knelt down, and he said a prayer before boarding his boat with his companions. Deacons of the church also went on board carrying lighted candles and a gold cross; and after crossing the river he venerated the cross, and then mounted his horse and went away, leaving behind in his monasteries about six hundred brothers in all.

'I, Bede ...'

Bede brings his *Historia Ecclesiastica* to its close with a modest auto-biographical note, followed by an invaluable bibliography of his own writings and a simple prayer of characteristic humility.

His brief paragraph — the eighth-century equivalent of the author biography on the dustjacket of a modern book — remains the core of what little we know for certain about the life of the Venerable Bede. There is a clear indication of his priorities in the comparative lengths of this autobiographical note and the list of his writings that follows it, because for Bede — we can be sure — his works were his life.

The bibliography, apparently complete at the time of writing in 731, has proved of inestimable value to modern historians, who have traced references to Bede's texts in later manuscripts and thus mapped the distribution of his works across Europe from the library of York to the court of Charlemagne. Here too is evidence of the scholar monk's wide range of intellectual interests — theology and biblical commentary, history and hagiography, poetry and the natural sciences. Bede's reference to his three works of science perhaps throws some light on the question of his attitude towards Wilfrid of Hexham. It was at the time of his ordination as priest in 703 that Bede wrote the first of his two books on chronology, his *De Temporibus*. This prompted a flurry of controversy when a member of Wilfrid's community at Hexham accused Bede of heresy. Although he was able to defend himself against the charges, we may wonder to what extent that exchange made its own contribution to Bede's personal feelings for Wilfrid's foundation and prompted the lack of warmth that coloured those pages in the *Historia*.

Bede lived for four years after the completion of his *Historia Ecclesiastica Gentis Anglorum*. Six decades after his passing came the savage Viking onslaught on the coastal monasteries of Northumbria. Looking now at Bede's own list of his life's work, we can only guess at how many of these manuscripts fell victim to that time of fire and sword.

✢

With the Lord's help, I, Bede, a servant of Christ and priest of the monastery of the blessed apostles Peter and Paul at Wiuraemuda and In Gyrwum, have composed this Ecclesiastical History of Britain, and of the English people in particular, using whatever information I could acquire from ancient documents, from the tradition of my elders, and from my own knowledge. I was born on the lands of this monastery, and at the age of seven was entrusted by the care of my family to the reverend Abbot Benedict, and then to Ceolfrith, to be educated. Since then I have lived my whole life in this monastery, devoting myself entirely to the study of the scriptures; and amid the observance of the discipline of the Rule and the daily task of singing in the church, it has always been my delight to learn, to teach or to write. I was ordained deacon at the age of nineteen and priest at the age of thirty, on both occasions through the ministration of the reverend Bishop John and at the bidding of Abbot Ceolfrith. From the time of my entering the priesthood until my fifty-ninth year, I have made it my business, for my own and my brothers' use, to compile brief notes on the holy scriptures extracted from the works of the venerable fathers, and to make additional comments to clarify their meaning and interpretation.

These are the commentaries:

The beginning of Genesis, as far as the birth of Isaac and the casting out of Ishmael: four books.
The Tabernacle, its vessels, and the vestments of the priests: three books.
The first Book of Samuel, as far as the death of Saul: four books.
The Building of the Temple, an allegorical interpretation like the others: two books.
The Book of Kings: thirty questions.
The Proverbs of Solomon: three books.
The Song of Songs: seven books.
Isaiah, Daniel, the Twelve Prophets, and part of Jeremiah: chapter divisions taken from the Treatise of St Jerome.

Ezra and Nehemiah: three books.

The Song of Habakkuk: one book.

The book of the blessed father Tobias, an allegorical interpretation concerning Christ and the Church: one book.

Also, chapters of Readings on the Pentateuch of Moses, Joshua and Judges; on the Books of the Kings and Chronicles; on the Book of the blessed father Job; on Proverbs, Ecclesiastes and the Song of Songs; on the prophets Isaiah, Ezra and Nehemiah.

The Gospel of Mark: four books.

The Gospel of Luke: four books.

Homilies on the Gospel: two books.

On the Apostle Paul I have transcribed in order whatever comments I found in the works of St Augustine.

The Acts of the Apostles: two books.

The Seven Catholic Epistles: one book each.

The Apocalypse of St John: three books.

Also, chapters of Readings on the whole of the New Testament, except the Gospels.

My writings also include:

A book of Letters to various people: one is on the six ages of the world; one on the dwelling-places of the children of Israel; one on Isaiah's words, 'And they shall be shut up in prison and after many days shall they be visited'; one on the principle of the leap year; and one on the equinox, after Anatolius.

Histories of the Saints: a book on the Life and Passion of St Felix the Confessor, which I put into prose from the metrical work of Paulinus; a book on the Life and Passion of St Anastasius, which had been badly translated from the Greek and amended even less well by some incompetent person, and which, as far as I could, I corrected to restore the meaning; and the Life of the holy father Cuthbert, monk and bishop, which I wrote first in heroic metre and later in prose.

A History of the Abbots Benedict, Ceolfrith and Hwaetbert, who ruled this monastery, in which it is my joy to serve our merciful Lord, in two books.

An Ecclesiastical History of our island and people, in five books.

A Martyrology of the festivals of the holy martyrs, in which I took care to note down all that I could find, including not only the date but also in what kind of combat and under what judge they overcame the world.

A book of Hymns in various metres and rhythms.

A book of Epigrams in heroic and elegiac metre.

A book on the Nature of the World, and a book on Chronology; also a longer book on Chronology.

A book on Orthography, set out in alphabetical order.

A book on the Art of Metre, and in addition another small book on Figures of Speech, or Tropes, that is, the figures and modes of speech woven into the language of the holy scriptures.

And I pray thee, good Jesus, that as Thou hast graciously granted me to drink with delight the words that give knowledge of Thee, so wilt Thou grant of Thy loving kindness that I may come at length to Thee, the fount of all wisdom, and stand for ever before Thy face.

AFTERWORD

'Hac sunt in fossa Baedae venerabilis ossa'

'In this tomb are the bones of the Venerable Bede' reads the epitaph carved on the slab of blue marble in the Galilee Chapel of Durham Cathedral.

Bede died on Ascension Eve in the year 735. He had been in poor health for some time, suffering from shortage of breath and swollen feet. He had not left the monastery at Jarrow for some two years, declining an invitation to make a further visit to his former pupil Egbert in York because of his failing health.

A letter written by the monk Cuthbert describes Bede still at work translating chapters of St John's Gospel into English on his deathbed. Cuthbert's account tells how Bede, almost at the point of death, learned that there were just a few lines left unfinished. He dictated the last lines of the translation in the moments before he drew his final breath.

Bede was buried in the south porch of the monastery, and his remains were later reinterred by the altar. The fame of his learning had already spread far beyond the frontiers of Northumbria, even in his own lifetime. Within fifty years of Bede's death, his cult had become firmly established. Alcuin was writing of Bede's relics achieving miraculous cures, and both Glastonbury in Somerset and Fulda east of the Rhine claimed to hold such relics.

Alcuin, the renowned monk of York who travelled through Europe to the court of Charlemagne where he became learned adviser and trusted confidant to the emperor, was born around the time of Bede's death. He was a pupil of Bede's pupil Egbert at York and played an important role in spreading Bede's works on the continent. Alcuin's numerous letters home survive as an invaluable source on Bede's growing fame, and it is from a letter of Alcuin that we learn of a copy of the *Historia* in the library of Offa, king of Mercia.

Bede's list of his own works in the last chapter of the *Historia* served as a publisher's catalogue and prompted the demand for more and more copies of his writings, placing the scriptorium at Wearmouth/Jarrow under ever greater pressure.

In a letter written to Bishop Lul of Mainz some thirty years after Bede, Abbot Cuthbert of Jarrow — the same Cuthbert who attended Bede's deathbed — apologizes for not sending all the copies of works of Bede requested by Mainz and explains that the winter weather had been so severe that the fingers of the monks were too stiff with cold to work on the copying of manuscripts.

Lul, like Alcuin, has his own interesting role in the spread of Bede's work on the continent. Alcuin is credited with bringing Bede's books to the court of Charlemagne, but Lul provides the link between Jarrow and Mainz. Originally a monk of Malmesbury who had studied at Jarrow, he travelled to the continent where he eventually succeeded Boniface as bishop of Mainz.

By the end of the eighth century, the golden age of Northumbria was nearing its end. Bede had expressed concern about the Saracen expansion into the Mediterranean, and yet it was not the militant Islam of the Saracens that was to bring about the end of Bede's Northumbria, but the dragon-ships of the northmen.

The first Viking raid on the English coast was directed at Lindisfarne in June 793 and the next year they struck at Jarrow. Undefended and richly endowed monasteries on exposed coastal sites offered irresistible prey for the warrior sons of Odin, just as the Britain abandoned by the Romans had tempted Bede's own Germanic forebears almost three hundred years before. As we have seen, the monks of Lindisfarne were forced to abandon Aidan's island and bear St Cuthbert's coffin to greater safety further inland.

Throughout the years of the Viking onslaught, Bede's bones were apparently undisturbed and so they remained until the second decade of the eleventh century, when a sacrist of Durham by the name of Alfred Westou paid a series of visits to Jarrow. An enthusiastic collector of holy relics, he removed Bede's remains and carried them back with him to Durham, where they were interred in Cuthbert's tomb.

During the episcopate of Bishop Hugh Puiset in the late twelfth century, Bede's remains were placed in their own silver shrine and carried in procession around the cathedral on the festivals of Ascension Day, Trinity Sunday and Whitsunday. In 1370 they were reinterred in the table tomb in the Galilee Chapel at the west end of the cathedral. Bede's ornate shrine did not survive the ravages of Henry VIII's dissolution, but his burial place was kept a secret. Today, Bede's tomb in the Galilee Chapel attracts a host of pilgrims and visitors as it has done down so many centuries.

Bede was finally confirmed as a saint and a doctor of the Church — the only Englishman to be honoured with that title — in 1899. His saint's day has long been celebrated in the church calendar on 27 May. Bede actually died on 25 May, Ascension Eve in the year 735, but as he died in the late evening after the first vespers of the Feast of Ascension, the day of his passing was recorded as Ascension Day. There was already a festival — associated with St Augustine — on the 26th and Bede's festival was postponed by twenty-four hours to the 27th.

It is a strange tradition that he is hardly ever referred to as 'Saint Bede' but is known today, as he has been for a thousand years, as 'The Venerable Bede.' 'Venerable' is a term of respect Bede himself often used to describe exalted individuals, kings as well as saints. In its modern usage it has connotations of great age, but that was not the sense in which it was used by Bede. The original meaning of 'venerable' was 'worthy of honour.' The title was first applied to Bede by the Council of Aachen in 836 and has remained with him ever since, with numerous tales of the miraculous offered to explain it.

Perhaps the most appealing such legend attaches to the carving of Bede's epitaph on the tomb at Durham. The monastic mason had carved 'Hac sunt in fossa Baedae ... ossa' and was undecided on the most suitable adjective to complete the inscription when he stopped work for the night. Returning to his task the following morning, he found the space he had left blank inscribed — presumably by an angelic hand — with the word 'venerabilis.' Thus was Bede celebrated in Cuthbert's great cathedral at Durham, while his fame spread throughout Christendom as 'the teacher of the whole Middle Ages.'

Bede is the only Englishman to be numbered by Dante among the worthies of his *Divine Comedy* where the poet places Bede between Isidore of Seville and the medieval mystic Richard of St Victor 'amongst the souls of the wise ... in the heaven of the sun.'

Of all the tributes paid to Bede, none have quite matched the extravagant eloquence of Notker Balbulus, monk of St Gall and biographer of Charlemagne, who, writing at the end of the ninth century, offers this resonant paragraph:

> God ... Who on the fourth day of creation brought forth the sun in the east, ordained in the sixth age of mankind Bede as a new sun in the west to illuminate the whole globe.

Chronology

Anglo-Saxon Northumbria

When Bede provided his own chronology for the *Historia*, his priorities were not always those of greatest value to today's reader. This chronology aims to provide a more useful modern perspective, following Bede's dates wherever there is any doubt, extending the period of Bede's chronology by sixty years, and adding dates of importance in Bede's personal history.

Entries printed in *italics* are those also included in Bede's chronology.

AD

547   *Ida established the kingdom of Bernicia at Bamburgh.*

565   *Columba arrived from Ireland to found his monastery on Iona.*

586   Aethelric became king of Bernicia.

593   Aethelfrith succeeded Aethelric to unite Bernicia and Deira as the kingdom of Northumbria on his marriage to Acha of Deira.

597   *Augustine arrived in Kent.* Death of Columba.

603   *Aethelfrith's victory at Degsastan.*

616   Aethelfrith killed in battle.
Edwin of Deira succeeded him as king of Northumbria.

627   *Edwin baptized by Paulinus.*

628   Birth of Benedict Biscop.

633   *Edwin killed. Paulinus and Queen Ethelburga returned to Kent.*
Aethelfrith's son Eanfrith became king of Bernicia.
Cadwalla of Gwynedd ravaged Northumbria.

634   Birth of Cuthbert. Eanfrith killed.
Oswald returned to defeat Cadwalla.

635   Aidan arrived from Iona to establish his monastery on Lindisfarne.

642   *Oswald killed in battle.* Oswy succeeded as king of Northumbria.
Birth of Ceolfrith.

651   *Oswin of Deira murdered on Oswy's orders.*
Death of Aidan. Cuthbert entered the monastery at Mailros.

655   *Penda of Mercia killed in battle on the river Winwaed.*

664   Council of Whitby. *Colman returns to Iona.*

670   *Death of Oswy.* Egfrith succeeded as king of Northumbria.

673   Birth of Bede.

674   St Peter's monastery at Wearmouth founded by Benedict Biscop.

679   Death of Etheldreda of Ely.

680 Bede entered the monastery at Wearmouth.
Death of Hild of Whitby. Death of Caedmon.

681 St Paul's monastery founded at Jarrow.

685 *Egfrith killed in battle.* Aldfrith succeeded.
Cuthbert became bishop of Lindisfarne.
Dedication of St Paul's monastery at Jarrow.

686 Plague at Wearmouth/Jarrow.

687 Death of Cuthbert.

689 Death of Benedict Biscop.

692 Bede ordained as deacon.

703 Bede ordained as priest.

705 *Aldfrith died.* Osred succeeded.

709 Death of Wilfrid.

716 *Osred killed.* Cenred succeeded.
Ceolfrith died at Langres on his way to Rome.

718 Cenred died. Osric succeeded.

721 Death of John of Beverley.
Bede completed his prose *Life of Cuthbert*.

729 *Osric died.* Ceolwulf succeeded.

731 Bede completed his *Historia Ecclesiastica Gentis Anglorum*.

735 Death of Bede on Ascension Eve, 25 May.

737 Ceolwulf resigned his kingdom to become a monk on Lindisfarne.

764 Ceolwulf died.

793 Viking attack on Lindisfarne.

794 Viking attack on Jarrow.

Genealogy

The Royal Houses of Northumbria

The following genealogical table has been restricted to those members of the royal houses of Deira and Bernicia prominent in Bede's histories or otherwise especially relevant to his narrative.

The genealogies of all Anglo-Saxon royal houses are notoriously complex and this table attempts to clarify the descent of Northumbrian kings rather than confuse the reader with a profusion of more obscure and less pertinent names.

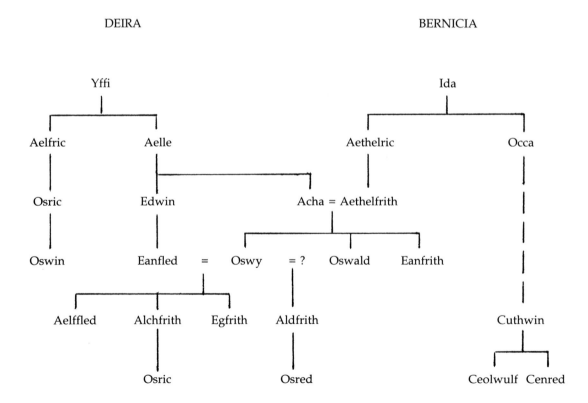

Glossary

Place names

Throughout this translation we have used the place names for towns, cities, villages or provinces that Bede himself used. Wherever Bede's place name refers to a town or other settlement to be found today, the modern name is included in this glossary. In those cases where the place Bede refers to has apparently disappeared, we offer the available informed guesses as to its modern counterpart.

In the case of permanent features of the landscape, effectively rivers, we have used the modern name in the translation, except in those cases of minor rivers which cannot be identified with certainty on modern maps. In those few cases again, informed guesswork is offered.

Aebbercurnig Abercorn, near Bo'ness, Lothian
Alcluith Dumbarton, Strathclyde

Beardaneu Bardney Abbey, Lincolnshire

Calcaria Tadcaster (?), North Yorkshire
Cale Chelles, near Paris
Cataracto Catterick, North Yorkshire
Coludesbyrig Coldingham, Lothian

Daltun Dalton-le-Dale, Durham
Dearmach Durrow, Louth
Denisesburn Rowley Burn, Northumberland
Derawuda, In Beverley, North Humberside
Dorciccaestra Dorchester-on-Thames, Oxfordshire

Eboracum York
Elge Ely, Cambridgeshire

Fresca, River unknown, probably in Northumberland

Gessoriacum Boulogne
Getlingum, In Gilling, North Yorkshire
Giudi possibly Inchkeith, Inveresk, or Stirling
Grantacaestir Cambridge
Gyrwum, In Jarrow, Tyne and Wear

Hacanos Hackness, North Yorkshire
Haethfelth Hatfield, South Humberside
Hagustaldesea Hexham, Northumberland
Hefenfelth Heavenfield, near Chollerford, Northumberland
Heruteu Hartlepool, Cleveland
Hii Iona
Hrofaescaestir Rochester, Kent
Hrypum, In Ripon, North Yorkshire

Inisboufind Inishboffin, off the coast of Galway

Laestingaei Lastingham, North Yorkshire
Lindsey Lincolnshire/South Humberside
Loidis Leeds, West Yorkshire
Lugdunum Lyons
Lugubalia Carlisle, Cumbria

Maeldum Meaux
Mag éo Mayo
Mailros Old Melrose on the river Tweed, Borders
Maserfelth Oswestry (?), Shropshire
Muig éo Mayo

Peartaneu Partney, Lincolnshire
Penneltun Old Kilpatrick, Strathclyde

Rutubi Portus Richborough (?), Kent

Sambuce unknown, possibly Cambois or Sandhoe, Northumberland
Streanaeshalch Whitby, North Yorkshire

Tuifyrdi, Ad Whittingham, Northumberland

Undalum, In Oundle, Northamptonshire

Verulamium St Albans

Wetadun Watton, near Beverley
White House Whithorn, Galloway
Winwaed, River unknown, probably a tributary of the Humber
Wiuraemuda (Monk) Wearmouth, Tyne & Wear

Anglo-Saxon tribal names mentioned by Bede

Gewissas   Original name for the West Saxons. The name was outdated by Bede's time, but later revived in the charters of Old English kings.

Gyrwas   Two East Anglian tribes living in the western fen country. The South Gyrwas lived around Ely.

Hwiccas   A tribe occupying territory in Gloucestershire, Worcestershire and western Warwickshire. At the time of Bede's reference, they were ruled by a sub-king under the overlordship of Mercia.

Continental provinces mentioned by Bede

Armorica   Brittany

Frisia   The Low Countries

Scythia   Bede probably meant Scandinavia, not the ancient Scythia north of the Black Sea.

Units of measurement used by Bede

hide   Anglo-Saxon unit of measurement of land based on the area necessary to support a household. The area varied from region to region. One hide ranged from 24 to 48 hectares (approximately 59 to 118 acres).

stades   Of Latin/Greek derivation, based on the length of a running track in classical times. Normally equivalent to 180 metres.

Bibliography

Works of Bede

Ecclesiastical History of the English People, ed. B. Colgrave and R. A. B. Mynors, Oxford 1969.

Baedae Opera Historica, ed. J. E. King, trans. after T. Stapleton, Loeb Classical Library, London 1930.

Venerabilis Baedae Opera Historica, ed. C. Plummer, Oxford 1896.

History of the English Church and People, trans. Leo Sherley-Price, Penguin Classics 1955.

Two Lives of Cuthbert, ed. B. Colgrave, Cambridge 1940.

The Age of Bede, ed. D. H. Farmer (includes prose *Life of Cuthbert* and *Lives of the Abbots*), trans. D.H. Farmer and J.F. Webb, Penguin 1983.

Bedas Metrische Vita Sancti Cuthberti, ed. W. Jaager, Palaestra 198, Leipzig 1930.

Other sources

Adair, John, *The Pilgrims' Way*, Thames and Hudson 1978.

Anderson, William, *Holy Places of the British Isles*, Ebury Press 1983.

Backhouse, Janet, *The Lindisfarne Gospels*, Phaidon Press/British Library 1983.

Bamford, Christopher, and Marsh, William Parker, *Celtic Christianity*, Floris Books 1986.

Blair, Peter Hunter, *Bede's Ecclesiastical History of the English Nation and its importance today*, Jarrow Lecture 1959.

——, *Northumbria in the Days of Bede*, Gollancz 1976.

——, *The World of Bede*, Secker and Warburg 1970.

Bonner, Gerald (ed.), *Famulus Christi*, SPCK 1976.

Browne, G.F., *The Venerable Bede, His Life and Writings*, SPCK 1919.

Campbell, James (ed.), *The Anglo-Saxons*, Phaidon Press 1982.

Colgrave, Bertram, *The Venerable Bede and his Times*, Jarrow Lecture 1959.

Coppin, Canon Ronald, *St Cuthbert's Heritage*, Durham: The Dean and Chapter 1987.

Cowie, L.W., and Gummer, J.S., *The Christian Calendar*, Weidenfeld and Nicolson 1974.

Cramp, Rosemary, *The Bede Monastery Museum*, St Paul's, Jarrow Development Trust 1980.

Fletcher, Eric, *Benedict Biscop*, Jarrow Lecture 1981.

Hill, David, *An Atlas of Anglo-Saxon England*, Blackwell 1981.

Kirby, D.P. (ed.), *St Wilfrid at Hexham*, Oriel Press 1974.

Knight, Stan, *Historical Scripts*, Adam and Charles Black 1984.

Laing, Lloyd and Jennifer, *A Guide to Dark Age Remains in Britain*, Constable 1979.

Lightfoot, Bishop, *Leaders in the Northern Church*, Macmillan 1907.

Magnusson, Magnus, *Lindisfarne*, Oriel Press 1984.

Nicolle, David, *Arthur and the Anglo-Saxon Wars*, Osprey 1984.

Ogilvy, J.D.A., *The Place of Wearmouth and Jarrow in Western Cultural History*, Jarrow Lecture 1968.

Parkes, M.B., *The Scriptorium of Wearmouth-Jarrow*, Jarrow Lecture 1982.

Proud, Kenneth, *Great Northern Saints*, Discovery Guides 1983.

Sawyer, P.H. (ed.), *Names, Words and Graves: Early Medieval Settlements*, University of Leeds 1979.

Stenton, Sir Frank, *Anglo-Saxon England*, Oxford University Press 1971.

Stranks, C.J., *The Life and Death of St Cuthbert*, SPCK 1964.

——, *The Venerable Bede*, SPCK 1955.

Ström, H., *Old English Personal Names in Bede's History*, Lund 1939.

Taylor, H.M. and J., *Anglo-Saxon Architecture*, Cambridge 1965.

Taylor, H.M., *English Architecture in the Time of Bede*, Jarrow Lecture 1961.

Thompson, A. Hamilton (ed.), *The Venerable Bede, his Life, Times and Writings*, Oxford 1935.

Wallace-Hadrill, J.M., *Bede's Ecclesiastical History of the English People — A Historical Commentary*, Oxford University Press 1988.

——, *Bede's Europe*, Jarrow Lecture 1962.

Wilson, David, *The Anglo-Saxons*, Pelican 1971.

Whitelock, Dorothy, *After Bede*, Jarrow Lecture 1960.

——, *English Historical Documents* c. 500-1042, Eyre and Spottiswoode 1955.

Index